TURNING IDEAS

INTO

BUSINESS

IF I COULD - YOU CAN !

—

by

Gary Thomas Murray

Gary Thomas Murray

Barcelona - Birmingham - Bogota

info@garythomasmurray.com

Dedication: I dedicate this book to all my business partners. All of you have taught me something, I can only hope I did likewise.

Contents

1. What's The Big Idea?

How Do You Get An Idea?

Lets not waist time just yet and get straight into it. I have a friend, let's say his name is Henry, as it actually is, and he has a head full of business ideas. Almost every time we meet he wants to tell me a new idea he has. In fact he even says he often can't get to sleep at night as his mind is working away on his latest idea.

I have another friend, we can call her Anna, as that's what her parents decided, and whenever we meet, which is not often enough, she always says how jealous she is of me and my ideas as she claims she never has a good idea for a business. Anna says she gets a little frustrated that she is always working for someone, be it Mercedes or Microsoft, she feels she can't break free. Later we will examine a little about whether Anna is better where she is or not, as yes, the grass does seem greener on the neighbor's side.

Now when Henry tells me some of his ideas, if I am honest I don't think they are that original or even workable. I actually think that on most occasions he would be far better served by going back to sleep rather than letting his mind get so pent up with his ideas. Ironically one of Henry's ideas was to introduce instant hot coffee in a can to Colombia, where upon opening the ting pull a small chemical reaction heats up the coffee within the can. This idea is ironic for two or three reasons, one it's a coffee idea keeping him awake, and I guess you got that irony by yourself.

Next you probably also realize that Colombia is a large producer of coffee, where most Colombians think they are the largest producer of the finest coffee in the world. I wont fact check everything in this book, but I can tell you they are not the largest or even second largest producer of coffee and I can also tell you that Costa Ricans, Brazilians, Jamaicans, Ethiopians and many others also feel they are produce the finest coffee in the world. I don't like coffee so I wont even hesitate an opinion here. What I can say however is that just the idea of coffee in a can in a coffee producing nation would be a hard sell, not impossible, but a hard sell.

The final reason I would say that Henry's coffee idea would be a hard business to pull off in Colombia is the fact that the minimum wage in Colombia is around 300$ US a month and hence the cost of a local cup of coffee in a local cafe or even from a street vender would be around 50 cents US. I did not research it when Henry mentioned his idea, but I would be pretty sure that the cost price of such a relatively sophisticated can of coffee, imported and put on the shelves of a supermarket would be at least as high if not higher than the same 50 cents.

Right there is a big barrier, as the canned coffee would cost at least twice as much as a quick coffee in a local cafe, which could be to go or a sit down comfortable one. Knowing the culture quite well due to my several years there, I would also say there is a culture of getting everything as cheap as possible and not really caring too much about high quality, so even a Starbuck's instant can of coffee would be a struggle. However, everything is possible and maybe with the right and expensive marketing and a little luck, which we all need, Henry could have been the next Juan Valdez, in a can!

So perhaps the first point to make is that yes there are certainly people who seem to have more ideas than others, but this does not indicate in any way shape or form the success of their ideas or the aptness of the person to drive their ideas forward into a business. It could be that my friend Anna would have been a great person to start and grow a business, even though she the original idea. It could also be that Henry was the worst person to start and run a business, even though he had many ideas. I'm not saying that's the case, but apart from good luck or bad luck, we can generally say the proof is in the pudding.

Hence, an idea is a very small part of a business. Yes its true that without an idea there is never going to be business in the first place and yes, you should feel proud if that idea was yours. However, I will hopefully show you that an idea can change so much, and generally needs to change so much, that the original idea almost becomes quite irrelevant during the process of starting a business. Think of it like your school exams that you did when you were eleven or even sixteen years old. There were important at the time and were a good platform for you later studies, but when you are looking for a new job at maybe twenty five or thirty years old, they are not really what count, instead everything you have done since then counts more.

A Good Or A Bad Idea

Are you or I best equipped in judging what makes a good business idea? I anyone a real expert when it comes to judging this? Maybe these television business angles have a special talent for knowing when something is going to work and when it's not? Well although it's natural for you to form your own opinion on anyone's idea, be it to do with business or otherwise, it is also best to keep an open mind and not to discourage someone too quickly. We need to keep in mind that most things in this life are possible.

As an example, let's say my friend Henry has forgotten about his instant hot coffee in a can idea and now has move on. He meets me for a coffee, in that original idea of Starbucks, and says to me his latest idea is now that he,

"Wants to open a new restaurant close to where we are sat".

So I naturally ask him,

"What kind of food will you sell?"

To which he replies

"Hamburgers"

I now think and possibly say to him,

"There are a lot of hamburger places around here already aren't there?"

"Yes." he says,

"But mine will be better."

Now instinctively I could think, as you would too no doubt, this is not a very original idea, and with all the burger chains out there already, how is he going to make this work? Surely he shouldn't bother; it's got failure written all over it. Apart from the well established competition, restaurants and bars are statistically the most popular businesses to do, as they are amongst the easiest to start up, but then they also close just as quickly as statistically speaking they generally fail faster than other businesses do.

However, I don't claim to be an expert investor or even an expert businessman, despite what writing this book may seem to signal, but I for one would not stamp on Henry's idea in this case. I am a firm believer, as you should be, that within the realms

6

of reason and legality, pretty much any business at all could be a success, yes even Henry's hot coffee can idea.

Thirty years ago who would have thought a wedding planner would even be a thing, let alone a successful business idea, or a spin doctor; would they have existed in more honest times, if those more honest times existed themselves. My point is, today there is a market for just about everything, everything is in the market and every one of us is in the market for at least something.

Let's take Henry's burger bar a little further; just to show you this book is not all about my ideas and me, although ultimately it really is. Let's take the worst possible case scenario and say he sets up business right across the road from McDonalds, and on top of that he's right next to Burger King too; how foolish would that be?

Well maybe not as foolish as you would first think. It is not exactly common knowledge, but can be seen first hand in many places that Starbucks do a similar thing in fact, and they seem to be doing ok for themselves. When Starbucks find themselves with a popular location, with a lot of throughput, they often open up another location within a hundred meters or so of the first one. You may think this is madness; they are competing with themselves, but not really. They are going after the "nearly's", the potential customers who did not want to cross the road, or did not want the wait faced at the first location, or perhaps wanted to make sure they got a seat, knowing in the first location all the seats are generally taken.

Lets examine; Henry would have his establishment, that's quite a posh word for a burger bar I know, in the middle of a proven area where people are already clearly buying burgers. This small amount of spying or research he would certainly have done before choosing his location. So right there he has potentially solved most businesses largest problem; how to get the word out about your business to potential customers. He has solved this problem by putting himself right there in front of his potential customers, those currently going to his competitors. Now all he needs to do is to get those potential customers to become actual customers.

Even still, you could think he was foolish; how will he get the customers of these giants in the burger industry into his establishment? Well curiosity is part of human nature, especially to the slightly younger of us and also part of our nature is to generally want something better than we already have. If it wasn't for this aspect of our nature, we would still be going around on horse and carts instead of in our Jaguar - I paces. Why else do we move house to a new and a better area? Is it really just for more space? Why do we go abroad for vacations? Why do we buy fashion or even men's health magazines?

Although many of us say we are happy with our jobs, our lives, houses, relationships and the like, we generally are still on the look out for improvements and we look for something better. And no, before you ask, I'm not divorced and hope never to be so. In fact I'm not even married, so that's a good or a bad start depending on your viewpoint.

So taking this to be true for most of us, and I generalize of course, if not then I will never finish this book, then most people who currently eat at the other burger places will at least wonder what the burgers are like at Henry's new place of business. That sense of wonder and the amount of it will then depend on Henry's ability to present his establishment in an attractive light to those that wonder. Perhaps if he presents his place as a similar fast food joint rather than a restaurant, maybe he will decrease the level of wonder.

Also, if his place looks unattractive for example, then his business is a tree already falling. However, if he perhaps presents it as a family owned business, maybe with his grandma's burger recipe and circular fries made from sweet potatoes, then there will be those that now wonder enough to wander right in there, I know I would, even if he wasn't a friend.

What Henry needs to do is not be afraid of his competition, but be confident and clever enough to compete with his competition. Both MacDonald's and Burger King are chain or franchise restaurants. Why does that matter? Well, it matters and Henry can benefit from this by highlighting his business as not being a chain. The owners of his competitors, the real founders of these chains, are not present at the locations. Those with the real business brains and the drive to make their businesses succeed are back at headquarters in the USA or more likely at their almost permanent holiday homes on the Bahamas or who knows where.

Well does this matter? Yes it does, it matters, as Henry will be at his place of business. It matters as his livelihood depends on the success of his place of business and it matters as he has all the flexibility possible to make his business work. Whereas his competitors are pre-programmed and can only offer the products they are told to offer from head office. They cannot react quickly or at all to anything Henry does, that's not how they work.

Another benefit is that Henry should be able to generate more respect from his employees and hopefully an attitude that you don't get at most chain restaurants, where it's more a case of going through the motions. Henry should be able to guarantee his employees give a much more friendly and personalized service to his customers by being there himself. This on top of a product menu a little more out of the ordinary compared to his competitors should stand Henry in good stead to not only compete, but to also beat his competitors. He just needs to differentiate his business and naturally give people a good product and then he will not have been so foolish as we all maybe thought after all.

So you see, the idea itself is not everything. You don't need a new groundbreaking money making scheme that no one has ever heard of in order for you to go into business. You can do something as simple as repeating an already existing business with perhaps a few variations to it. I would not however, start a business just for the sake of it; it is not something to be taken lightly. You certainly need to have great ambition and be prepared to either be very lucky or very determined, or hopefully even both of these. For sure you can do it, putting aside the idea for the moment, but the first real decision comes in deciding is this really something you want to do.

Having said this, I don't necessarily think everyone is suited to starting and running a business. Maybe my other friend Anna, who says she never gets any ideas, is just as well without those ideas and just as well without her own business. She is a very successful corporate businesswoman in her own rights and has a successful career. Sometimes, many times in fact, this can be just as rewarding, if not more so, than starting a business. I say this, as there are far more content employees out there than there are business owners. Ultimately you have to do what you believe will make you happy and not worry too much over not having your own business. Having your own business brings its own level of stress, which can be far higher than being an employee and it may simply not be for you.

What Were My First Business Ideas?

Throughout my twenties I don't believe I ever entertained the idea of starting a new business, at least not with any seriousness. Furthermore I don't believe I would have had much to offer to a new business at that stage as I was really just developing as a person myself and I don't even think I have finished that process yet.

I do remember I liked working with older more experienced people as I always felt they had something to teach me. They often taught me things through their stories and also through their actions. I was like a sponge, soaking up as much of their experiences as possible. The way others behave can often teach you how you should behave, but it's also important to have your moral compass out of your jacket pocket. Sometimes you need to stop and look at yourself and learn from what you are actually doing yourself, is it right or is it wrong.

During this time I cant recall ever even having an idea for a business. After my years at university I was more worried about making money and maybe my own moral compass was not always pointing due north. Expense reports, now they bring back memories and not from the news headlines surrounding British and no doubt almost every other countries politicians.

At my first real job as an intern for British Gas there was an unfortunate culture of trying to get away with what you could. Their employees were not alone though as you often hear stories about other industries such as the UK car plants where so many spare parts were stolen that the workers could almost have set up a whole other assembly line. This culture was and probably still is ashamedly true in most industries where the parts of products are easy to sell on.

As our off site British Gas office was far away from the headquarters, we had the right to claim for a daily lunch. Here I can certainly remember claiming for many lunches that I never ate;

by putting a receipt and claim form in for food I never bought was a way to supplement my income and at the time I didn't feel too guilty as most others were doing the same or worse than that. Not everyone, but many of us took advantage. You may think I'm getting off the point and you would be right, but I do now feel ashamed of my actions in what amounts to petty theft from my employer and I think its worth mentioning our own ethics, whether we work for ourselves or for other people. Taking advantage is really nothing to be proud of and it's hardly a good example to set.

Perhaps this serves to highlight that I was not ready to start a business, not a legitimate one at least. Steeling time, money, goods or simply just not putting the effort you should put into your job should be an indication to anyone that you are perhaps not ready to go it alone. How can you expect anyone that works for you to be honest and put their full effort in if you yourself don't.

Still off the point, I remember a boss I had at my next job after teacher training. His surname was Cross, and that was a very fitting name indeed. This man was very successful and with a group of other men he had left one company with a new idea developed for them and had formed another company with this new product. The second company set up in direct competition to the first company and eventually became a multi million-dollar success.

However, this man was possibly the rudest person I have ever met. I recall being at a hotel bar one night and they were closing as it was about 2am, but this man did not want to accept that they would close while there were customers still sat there. He said some pretty appalling things to the waitress and the guy behind the bar for which there was no excuse, not even being drunk, as he quite possibly was.

Here you have a small example of how power and success can go to your head and you can become something you perhaps never thought you would or could become. If I ever saw myself becoming so bad tempered and rude to people in that way, I think I'd prefer not to have ever started a business in the first place. So as I said, you also need to learn from people what not to do. We all hear stories of movie starts and their bad treatment of others; well it's also true of businessmen, politicians and any position of power.

So back off my tangents and returning to my first real business idea. I had just left my MBA course at ESADE business school in Barcelona, a beautiful city although not without its downsides, but there again what location isn't? After I left the course I met a fellow student, who by coincidence was also English, but he was not exactly on the same course as myself. He was there with his wife with whom he had fallen in love with and got married in the space of just a few months, if I remember correctly; how lucky I thought to myself.

One day when we were cycling around the Barceloneta area of the city, and this is back around 15 years ago now, he said,

"There must be a way to get money out of these foreigners that come to Barcelona."

This was back at a time when the economy in Barcelona was rocketing, everyone wanted to be in Barcelona. The weather, the beach, the food, the architecture, the good looking people, what more could you possibly want? It was certainly a time when a lot of investment was coming in, when many tech businesses like the UK's lastminute.com were setting up their servers there. It's not really a chapter for this book, but let's say the Catalan government was making it very tempting for businesses and their employees to base themselves in Barcelona. A bit similar to the way they made it attractive for many football players to go there also, in terms of tax treatment.

I'm not criticizing, as I am sure many governments have done similar things and without these kind of special treatments I guess there would be no UK car industry at all today and when I talk about the UK car industry I talk about foreign firms such as Nissan, Ford, Honda, BMW and the likes making some of their cars in the UK. The special treatment Margaret Thatcher gave these companies to attract them in the first place and no doubt the promises Mrs. May is giving to them now in regards to how things won't change after Brexit, are probably the main reasons the UK has something of a manufacturing base at all.

So yes, there was a lot of money coming into Barcelona and hence, property prices were rising at maybe the highest level ever seen there. Just on that point, and to still avoid getting to my real point, we can show a little of the luck element in business and life. Around this time and in Barcelona I bought my first ever property and even now, about 12 years later that property is still not worth what it was when I bought it. All my school friends had bought property several years before me and had seen huge rises in value, but it just goes to show, you do need a little luck, or at least a lack of bad luck.

Back to it, so what was my first idea, my very first business idea? Silly as it may seem, it was simply to rent jet skis out to tourist in Barcelona. Yes, I'm serious, I even ran some numbers and it was looking quite good at that early and enthusiastic stage. A second hand jet ski would have cost about 2000 euros and thirty minutes would run at about 75 euros. Less petrol costs, storage, transport and the likes, but still that's not very long to get you're invested capital back and then be making money hand over fist, I thought. Couple that with the idea of only having to work about half the year or less and it was quite appealing.

My new potential partner was also interested, as we again cycled around by the Barcelonetta area of the city; that's basically down close to where the manufactured beach area is that tourists love, but the Catalan's generally avoid. However, it didn't take long to see that this idea was a none starter. Due to a few deaths in Spain's other areas coastal areas on jet skis the regulations to rent and operate them had become quite stringent. The vehicles would need to have a safety cut out operated from land and they could not come within a certain distance of the beach. In reality the authorities of Barcelona would never permit jet skis close to their beloved city and rightly so, what a racket they would have made, enough to scare the tourists off.

What next then? Well the same basic idea of getting money from foreigners visiting Barcelona changed and developed, which is often what needs to happen! It's important in business to keep an open mind and let yourself be guided by many factors, mainly by customers needs. If you can actually create that customer need, or expose it, all the better. So the next idea was not such a huge stretch from renting jet skis to tourists, the next idea I came up with was renting another popular Barcelona transport to tourists, little 50cc motos or scooters.

I'm not sure if there are more motos than cars in Barcelona, someone can google that, I'd say there are not, but there are a lot and they are very handy, especially in terms of getting ahead of the traffic and in terms of parking, which is difficult and terribly expensive in Barcelona. So as they already do on many Asian and Mediterranean islands, I thought that renting motos would be a good idea for Barcelona as no one was currently doing that there.

At this point I started to think not just about tourists, but also about the many students living in Barcelona. I was using my own experience on the MBA course to see a need that existed; having this personal experience is both useful and important. From where I lived in my shared and rented accommodation it took me from door to door about fifty minutes to get to school and another fifty minutes to get home. That's well over one and a half hours wasted each day and this when I had a lot of MBA material to get through. We were often at school from 8am to 9pm. I estimated that on a moto I would have done the journey in about fifteen minutes each way, or even ten at a push and if the lights where in my favor, saving me 1 hour and twenty minutes a day!

Thus far you can see that none of my ideas are that original as such; they already existed, albeit in different countries. At the moment you could, if you like, even say that both my ideas were foolish, but I'm only trying to highlight the process and its not finished yet. My new partner for one did like my moto idea. He had another idea to do with motos / scooters, I think it was selling seat covers as many of them you see on the streets are ripped and he in fact was a motorbike fan; I was not.

So we looked into the idea of renting motos to tourists, but more so to students and we worked out monthly and daily tariffs and despite you maybe thinking it foolish, it did made sense financially; it could in fact work.

At this stage I really wanted to stay in Barcelona and I just needed some income to be able to do so. I had some savings to invest, not much, about 35,000 euros or so, but that would get us a good few motos along with my partners savings from the house they had sold in the UK. Yes this couple were so convinced on the idea of setting up a business in Barcelona that they had sold their UK house and everything. I even remember helping them with their furniture when it arrived and lifting it all several flights of stairs.

So what went wrong with this business idea? One word, insurance. We could not find an insurance company willing to insure the motos against theft, which in Barcelona there is an awful lot of in terms of motos. I was pretty sure most customers would not be willing to have an excess on their rental contract for the cost of the actual moto itself and hence, we wrote that idea off also, a little insurance joke there. In hindsight, I don't think we actually looked that hard into the insurance side and maybe we only contacted one provider, which is ridiculous, but without wishing to lay blame the insurance quotes were not on my list of duties, okay so I am laying the blame.

In any case, not many years later another couple of students from a competing MBA school did set up that business, so either things changed in the insurance markets or they worked a bit harder at the idea than we did. This business is still around today illustrating that my idea was not so foolish as it perhaps seemed.

Sometimes that's what it comes down to, determination and not giving up at the first hurdle. Looking back at it now, we could have provided our own insurance in terms of insurance is just a numbers game. We could have sold a basic insurance with the moto rental estimating that a certain number of motos would be stolen during the year, and hence basing our insurance premiums on that, quite easy really!

At this stage and after two ideas and having got nowhere, it would have been easy to give up, but my mind was still pretty active and I was still determined to stay in Barcelona, to learn more Spanish than just that required to order a plate of food. Although still hopeful of business success I went and got a part time job. I started teaching GMAT, the exam you have to do before getting into a business school. It didn't pay that much, but at least they didn't take any tax from my wages. Spain is or was certainly not back then, quite up to scratch in going after those who avoid tax. I often think that in Southern Europe things are a little different to the North, something which Greece and Portugal highlighted, although Ireland was in a similar boat and that's pretty Northern.

In fact, I will always remember when I purchased my first property mentioned above. I was at the bank that was providing me with the mortgage and there I sat in a boardroom with the sellers, the notary and the bank representative. Suddenly in the middle of this meeting where we would sign off and I would pay the money, the notary got up and walked out of the room for five or ten minutes.

"What's going on here?" I thought.

I was quickly explained this was the time when you pay the part of the transaction avoiding that avoided state tax, i.e. the time when you pay the black money. This was common practice in Spain, although at that stage it had been reduced from avoiding half of the tax to maybe just a quarter. I make no comment as to whether it still continues today, but in the UK and the USA it certainly doesn't happen and if it did, you'd be in jail for it.

Anyway, there I was with still no workable business idea forthcoming. Was it possible that we were not cut out for this, that maybe it's not as easy as we thought it would be? Maybe I would have to go back and continue working in one company or another for the rest of my days. It had still only been about one or two months though, so no, I was not giving up yet, so on and upwards.

My next idea was a time relevant idea, i.e. it was something needed at that time, but that's not needed today. Back then most tourists or business travellers coming to Europe from the USA or Asia would simply not be able to use their cell phones anywhere in Europe. If you are old enough to remember the phrase tri-band or later quad-band phones, well at that time those phones hardly existed and so a travelling business man or tourist travelling abroad would generally be incommunicado in terms of their cell phone.

Hence, my idea was simple, we would rent cell phones to those that needed them. We could provide them at the airport or at hotels and we would collect them there also. The business would involve the packaging, delivery and collection of the phones, the billing and the charging of these customers. One downside would be that with the mobile phone billing technology back then, we could only charge the customer after they had left the country since we would not know how much they had spent before that point. This was not ideal, although with credit cars we could of course take a decent size deposit.

Yet again we did some numbers and we could theoretically make it work. In fact, it was a business that already existed in London's Heathrow airport and seemed to be working well. However, I was already loosing faith in my own idea to be honest. It seemed very labor intensive and for not a huge profit at the end of the day. So once again, we were heading back to square one, was I ever going to come up with a workable idea?

Quit Your Day Job Or?

Very briefly it is worth looking at this, although with everyone's personal circumstances varying so much, it's perhaps hard to give any definitive advice. In my own case I had left my MBA and I had no other full time job, so there was no decision to make in terms of whether to leave one or not. I did take a part time job to perhaps keep me sane and make some money, but there was not that much of a time commitment here.

For most people with an idea to start their own business they will normally be in full time employment. I would say on the one hand that the idea of trying to start a business in this position is like the idea of trying to work during the day and study at night. This is exactly what I had to do as a tax consultant and while it can be done, it leaves you with virtually no life at all. It also means you cant fully put your effort into either one thing or the other.

However, many people do it and in terms of your own and families security, it is certainly worth making this sacrifice for a while, at least until you have done your research and are confident enough to believe your idea has credence. You can do a lot of the development of the idea while still in full time employment, of course you can.   If anything, initially your idea should be something of a hobby; something you enjoy spending your time involved with and thinking about.

It never looks good to chop and change jobs in the big picture, so before you ever resign, I would do as much work as you can on your idea. Speak to as many people as you can and yes I repeat myself, as I will a lot in this book, develop it as much as possible before you give up your guaranteed monthly income and benefits package.

2. Developing An Idea

Although I didn't realize it at the time, but everything I had done up until now was the development of an original idea. The basic premise of the idea was to be able to provide foreigners in Barcelona with some kind of service that they would pay us for. I had gone from renting jet skis, to renting motos and then on to renting cell phones. All the time reasoning with myself and then with my partner regarding the viability of each proposal.

This for me is the most fun part of starting a business. It's perhaps akin to planning a holiday or choosing which new car to buy. The process of choosing and imagining is almost more fun than the actual driving of the car or being on the actual holiday; I think we all know the idea of something can often be better than the reality. Eating a whole packet of chocolate biscuits is another example where the reality never quite lives up to the idea.

What do I mean by developing an idea? Well there are two things for me, but there maybe other things for you. Firstly an idea is often just one sentence or even just a couple of words. This in itself is not a business, far from it in fact. There are many more stages that would then need to follow in order to make the business a reality and figuring all those things out is for me developing the idea.

For example, Henry's idea of starting a burger bar was originally just a thought, an idea. Then he had to think what kind of burgers, cheap and cheerful, boutique style ones, or family recipe. Location had to be thought as well as how to get the customers through the doors, which in this case was very much related to the location he chose. All this, a quite limited process in his case, was development of the idea.

The other side of an idea's development I referred to, which is perhaps more fun, is when the idea possibly won't work as it is planned. Maybe it won't make enough money as there are not enough customers, or perhaps costs are too high even prohibitive. Here the idea itself needs developing or shifting or morphing into something else, this part for me is quite fun.

It's often the case that people will tell you your idea wont work, sometimes without even really understanding it or dedicating any time to think about it. I have a friend who almost always tells me my ideas won't work, but then I when I research a little more I generally find someone else already doing the same thing, so then I can see it could have worked and that this person is simply not the right person to go to for encouragement.

When someone tells you your idea won't work, you really need more than that; you need that person to be analytical enough to tell you why won't it work. You don't need someone that can only think if the idea will work for them. You need them to get outside their box and see the potential needs of others.

If they still see problems with the idea, and they explain what they are, then you need now to try to fix this or that problem. You need to be good at thinking outside the box, but you must accept that by fixing this or that problem, you may then create other problems. However, if the other problems you have created are smaller than the original problem, then you have in fact progressed, you have started to develop your idea.

Now you move on and try to fix the smaller problems one by one and possibly make other even smaller problems as a result. Eventually you can hope to make the problems so small or none existent that your idea will actually work!

To see this in practice let's go back to the last version of my idea; renting cell phones to foreign business people or tourists. The problems I had mentioned were the delivering and collection of the phones, would the hotels really help us in this or would it all have to be done at the airport. Also the fact that the customers would be out of the country when their bill came was not ideal and I did not like the risk associated with all this. Could I solve these problems or could I eliminate them in the first place?

Well, one night in bed, while my housemates were having a party, I had a brain wave, an epiphany moment even. And yes I know, quite sad that I was not interested in being involved in said party, but there you go you cant start a successful business and be a party guy, well I'm sure you can actually. Anyway, I can remember the brain wave moment it to this very day and I wanted to tell someone about it there and then, but I had to wait, as it was way past midnight and anyone I was interested in telling was not at the house party and was in fact asleep.

The epiphany that had come to me was so simple in the end and it had been right there in front of my eyes from the very start. Why would we want to rent cell phones to foreigner business travellers and have all the associated logistical problems and risks that came with this, when there was another group of foreign people that needed local cell phones and these people were far easier to service. In fact some of this very group were at that moment getting hammered on sangria in my apartment. This group was of course the very same foreign MBA students to which I belonged.

These foreign and adult students with no income or credit history in Spain were not very welcome customers for the three large cell phone companies in Spain at that time. In fact, in order to get a contract you often had to leave a large deposit and for many nationalities, they simply did not give cell phone contracts at all. Hence, most students, including myself, ended up with prepaid phones, which meant there were no discounted handsets and calls were not that cheap either. It also often meant credit running out in the middle of a call and having to go out to a shop to add more credit late at night or in the rain.

This was quite some time ago of course, things have moved on a bit since then. These days you can have a "prepaid" service and yet the phone company still takes the money directly out of your account each month, which to me means it's more of a contract than a prepaid service, but what do I know.

You may ask why had I not thought of that before and there is a simple answer to that question, and one that does not involve me admitting I was stupid. The answer in actual fact is that it had never occurred to me that we would be able to set up a company and provide regular long-term mobile phone contracts. Up until now we had been talking about very short-term contracts, where we would really just be re-selling our own normal contracts that we have with the providers. In fact, even though the moment felt like a huge breakthrough, I did not actually know if the Spanish providers would indeed allow us to do what I intended to do.

Even still I felt confident and with this one change in direction, this one development I had managed to eliminate most of the problems with renting phones out to tourists. The only problem remaining now would be that the billing would still be after the months end, but this was not such an issue as the customers would still be in Spain, at least until their MBA or Masters course finished a year or two later.

I think my partner liked the change I proposed although he did not see how we would make money without charging very high prices compared to other contracts. However, I took control of that side and I worked very hard to find us some contacts at two of the large providers in Spain at the time, Orange and Movistar. I arranged a couple of exploratory meetings with them and the wheels were in suddenly motion.

Not All Ideas Work Out

Now lets move on to another idea I worked on, its not one I'm particularly proud of, but I think it's just as important to learn from failures as it is from successes. The main point to see is that ideas should develop and not be fixed and even bogged down under their own weight. However, not all ideas are going to work, no matter how much they develop and no matter how good you think they may be. If they did, then everyone would be in business for themselves.

While in Colombia, South America, and not just for a short vacation, I had time on my hands and so with a friend I made there, we started throwing around a few ideas. This is long after my mobile phone business was up and running. This friend had an interest in automobiles and had been head of sales for BMW and for a 4x4 off road vehicle company also, so its fair to say his mind was directed towards this kind of market sector.

I'm not quite sure how we got to there and I certainly must accept some of the blame, but we started to look at paramotors, or paragliding with a motor attached. This was something relatively new and we thought it would be a hit where we were with so many outdoor areas to explore around Colombia. Cleary you may not want to explore the terrorist occupied areas, or the coco growing fields, but even leaving them out, many families owned countryside properties.

During the investigations, it seemed quite safe and something that was easy to do, or at least that's what the companies that make these units and organize events would like you to believe. The initial outlay would not be that high and running costs would be quite reasonable, since it was basically only a parachute with a very small engine attached.

There would be the option to import and sell them or import them and rent them out, we were quite open to the options. In reality this was never going to be a get rich quick scheme or a multi million-dollar business, but it was something to do more than anything for me and I could see us making money.

Now my idea here was not to start the business and keep it for years and years. The idea was to get it started, show it could make some decent money and then sell it on as a going concern. In order to do this, you obviously need to be able to show profit and potential. In fact, I would have been quite happy in simply importing the units and letting others organize the events themselves as that seemed a bit time consuming to me.

However, after further investigation, and investigation is always important, I found quite a few accidents online and read that it was not so easy to fly these apparatus as it first appeared. Hence, without investing too much more time we moved quickly moved away from this idea and looked for another one. This is the development that is always fun but sometimes frustrating and it's an area where you need some insight and a lot of common sense.

It's not a stretch to say this basic idea developed, i.e. the idea of importing some motor powered device for recreational use and we did not give up. We stuck around a similar market and I then came up with the idea of importing Hovercrafts. You may be saying already that's a stupid idea, but be careful, as although it may have been a stupid idea, many stupid ideas make people millionaires. Although granted, this one was possibly not going to test that theory.

Still with the large percentage of people having second homes, more farm type like properties, a hovercraft could have been something quite interesting for these people to have fun on their land with. I contacted some manufactures in the US and got some pricing back and at that point that I could see this would also be quite difficult to make work as a business. Its one thing spending 1000 US $ on a fun weekend device, its another thing spending as much as a second hand car; Colombia is still a poor country after all.

Hence, this idea did not get off the ground either, nor the water in this case, but it would have been great fun! So once again we were back at square one. My friend then had the idea to import these 3-wheeled motorbikes, the ones with very fat tires that handle the corners almost like a car. Certainly they looked good fun, but import taxes would also put them into a very elite market and it really is a quite young persons vehicle of choice, so again our potential client base would be limited.

However, an almost logical path now took us to kit cars; which are something of a specialty of the UK since they used to be a way for car companies to avoid having to charge purchase tax (VAT) back in the 1960's. I'd always liked classic cars and had a few when I was younger, fresh out of University, so this was more entering my area of interest and as the companies were generally based in the UK, well again it worked for me.

We contacted the larger of these kit car companies, Caterham, about the possibility of importing their cars to South America. They answered and were interested, but they were already in talks with another group that were trying to do the same thing in Bogota. Perhaps this already existing interest spurred our interest on further, although the other group had more of a business plan than we did and they were actually going to import these cars to create a race series with them. At the time we did not know any of this of course.

We were too slow off the mark with Caterham and we would not have competed with this other group anyway, as they invested quite heavily in the business, around a million dollars was their starting capital. It was a wealthy family who already had various car dealerships and the son of this family was going to head this business, with his parent's money backing him up of course.

Most businesses in Colombia are those that are passed down within families and those that already have family money mostly start up even new businesses like this. There is big class divide in the country that makes it difficult for the lower classes to get somewhere or indeed anywhere in life, in my opinion.

Still, as we were now pretty sure that these kit cars could sell the Colombia, just by the fact that Catherham were going to be sold there, I looked for other manufacturers and found the nemesis of Caterham, The Westfield Sports Cars Group. Their location was only about forty-five minutes from where I used to live in the UK and so it was not hard to get in touch and visit them. They were of course happy to sell their cars into new markets and so they would be happy to have us as their Colombian distributors. They also knew of Caterham's ventures in the same country and told me they were shipping twenty of their cars out there.

Again, this news gave me growing confidence in just how popular these cars could prove to be out there in Colombia; Caterham had already sold twenty after all. Pretty much with this my partner and I decided to invest in two cars and ship them over from the UK to Colombia. We would be 50 / 50 partners and my friend had also filled me with confidence that he knew enough people from his days working in the automobile industry that he could get the vehicles shipped and imported and registered with no problem at all.

Now if we pause for a moment, you may already be able to see some errors in the development of this business idea? I was making two mistakes at this point already. The mistake with regards to my partner we will discuss in the next chapter. The other mistake that you maybe spotted was that I really had not done too much investigation. Yes it was great information that Caterham were sending twenty cars to Colombia as this surely meant that they had or believed they could sell them. This by itself lead me to believe that we too could sell our cars since they were basically the same and were cheaper.

However, I let myself get carried away lets say in that I did not investigate who were buying these cars and why. I did no real research into the sports car market in Colombia at all, relying instead on my partner's positive thinking about how easy it would be to sell these cars.

As I mentioned, Colombia is a terribly divided country between the rich and the poor, far more so that any other country I have lived in and yes I did live there. I really should have looked into the very small circle of people that could afford these men toys and seen how easy or not they would be to sell.

In the UK, where they were made, we have many old airfields that are converted into racetracks. If we just look at the major circuits in the UK, which provide services for track days, you have twenty circuits, that's virtually more than the rest of Europe put together. After this there are a further twenty or even thirty smaller tracks where you can also drive your weekend toy or weekday work car like a lunatic if you choose. Track days are quite big business in the UK now which is great for car fans and the UK is certainly as big a car enthusiast country as anywhere.

Colombia on the other hand? I did not even know at this point how many tracks the country had or how they worked. My idea was to sell the cars for road use, so perhaps track days were not high on my mind, but I certainly should have been more thorough in looking into this! Bogota, with ten million inhabitants, has just one realistic track for enjoying these cars to their limits and this track is not so easy to go whenever you please either. Due to the unfortunate death a few years ago of the son of an important person in the car circle over there, the track had almost stopped offering track days for individuals.

What my partner and I did also not realize, and we really should have looked much deeper into it, was that this wealthy family who were importing about twenty cars from Caterham were actually starting their own race series. This is why they were bringing so many cars across to Colombia. These people had no intention of using them on the public roads, just on the one racetrack and in an exclusive series for these cars!

Suffice to say, this business idea really did not work for us. It was a bit naive and I accept my part of the blame for not really looking into it enough. I treated it more as a hobby rather than anything else and I guess I got what I deserved.

Sometimes you do make mistakes and you simply need to fix them if you possibly can, learn from them, which you always can, and move on. If you manage to get out without loosing too much capital and instead just loose your time, then you have not done too badly. There can be things against you and timing is often everything, but sometimes you simply make bad decisions and you have to know when to move on, which again we will look at later.

I can laugh about this business now, but Catherham also have various cars unsold and that is with all the contacts their owners in the in the car industry and within the elite potential customers. If out of a bad situation you can take something positive, then that's not too bad is it? I for my part took 4000 km of driving a hugely fun car around a country I never dreamt I would even visit, let alone live in. I rekindled my interest in cars and more so in driving them, so I cant complain too much about it.

Just Do It?

Well yes, but it also depends on the ease with which you can do it and also on the overall risk involved in doing it. There is no secret in having ideas, they come or they don't, but once you get one, you do need to be prepared to let it flow, let it change and don't be too rigid with it. The one thing that is for sure is that if you just keep the idea in your head, it will never go anywhere else. It will never have the chance to see the light of day and less chance to be successful.

Virtually all ideas need some development; only a fool would say they don't. You can ask how do you know when it is developed enough. The answer is possibly never, as a good business will always continue to develop, but,

"How do you know when it is enough to take the idea and make a business from it?"

That's a similar question to how do you know when you should ask your girlfriend or boyfriend to marry you. Its something you just know, or you take a leap of faith. What's the worst that can happen?

That last question is quite interesting in fact and brings to mind many other factors, which I will briefly mention in the hope of getting you out there with your idea. I can't stress enough this step of getting your idea out of your head and into the real world. Be that discussing it with friends, doing some investigation, surveys, or studying similar businesses, but do something. Don't wait for the perfect idea as it does not exist, the same as the perfect man or woman does not exist.

With that in mind, going back to the previous question, I always find it useful to look at the worst-case scenario. If you were going to have an affair outside of your marriage, not that I for one second suggest you do, what is the worst that can happen. Well, quite simply, the worst that can happen is your partner finds out, they rightly get very upset and they divorce you and take you to the cleaners. Maybe you even loose custody of your children; this is the worst-case scenario.

This is what you have to ask yourself before you make that move, is it worth it? I would say it's never worth it in that case! In fact, off at a slight tangent, but if I know a man or a woman to be unfaithful, and in my Colombian experience I can say I knew quite a few, then I can also say this person is probably not good to do business with and certainly not to be the a partner of.

Why? Quite simple really, if this person is unfaithful, then they are clearly dishonest and have few scruples. If they are prepared to lie to the person they care most about in this world, then what on earth makes you think they wont lie to you. Why would you trust this person when they have shown themselves to be untrustworthy to others? I learnt this lesson a little late I guess, but maybe it will be useful to you, especially when it comes to selecting business partners, which we will talk about next.

Back to the current point, worse-case scenario. If the business idea is the hamburger bar Henry wanted to open, then what is his worst case if it fails? Well, that's not hard to work out. You need to look at the amount he would need to invest to revamp the establishment, salaries, overheads and all other costs for a certain time frame, including the rent. If the business is a terrible failure, his worst case is to loose this investment, or to loose someone else's money, if he had investors etc.

Maybe some investment can be recuperated by selling to someone else whom values the remodeling work put in and will pay for it, but that would not be worse case, that maybe second worse case. On the other hand, if Henry or if you have an idea which is an online business and the only investment is in setting up an app or a website and then some marketing, then no doubt your worse-case scenario wont be so bad, you should have spent less than in the case of the Burger Bar.

For my part, most of my ideas, apart from the kit cars above, are based on very little investment. They are more service based companies than manufacturing or physical product based companies. This gives the advantage that these companies generally depend on my effort rather than anything else and hence in my case, the worst that can generally happen is that I waste several months of my time if the idea falls flat on its face.

This is worth thinking about when you think of starting your own business. Before you invest your own savings or somebody else's, is there a way to maybe test the water first? Try and be slightly cautious here and so even if this idea fails to make it as a business, you may well still be able to try another idea later, not having lost everything you have. This is better than being so badly burnt that you simply wont want to put your hand in the water again.

3. Partnership Or Go It Alone?

We've all heard the popular and possibly true saying,

"You only really get to know your partner when you get divorced from them."

This is possibly a bit unfair in terms of marriages though as I don't think it's just the divorce that is the big factor here, but instead the reasons behind the divorce. If your partner had two other partners that you didn't know about, then I think you would be quite justified in changing your opinion and hence behavior towards them and yes they may then see a side to you they had not seen before.

Also for many people when there is money involved it tends to complicate things further and well, children, they can be dragged into situations they should not be. However, lets go back to business partnerships, at least there tend not to be any children there. Having said that, starting your own business can be like having a child that you raise and nurture and hence, you can become quite attached to it; it is your life's dream after all!

While a business is simply a dream, and contrary to what Disney may tell us, most dreams don't come true, then perhaps its not as important than when your dream is real and money is coming in. If a business fails before it gets off the ground, it's not such a big surprise and certainly won't hurt as much as if it had already succeeded before then failing. Maybe if an awful lot of work had gone into it and money had been spent, then yes this changes things a little.

They say, and you will find the statistics do back it up, that most partnerships fail within even the first year or two. I personally think that if there is to be a partnership in business then it makes more sense for it to be between more than just two people. This way at least there can be a vote and the majority can decide rather that just having one against the other. One has to accept that if all the others are against your line of thinking then maybe your thinking is not quite spot on in this case.

Yes an even number of partners could still lead to a split vote, but the simple probability of that or of a very strange suggestion causing a large discussion is less likely. Maybe this way friendships can be preserved and besides, theoretically less money would need to be invested by each person.

Lets get straight back to my mobile phone idea and the partnership that was forming with my new English friend. My idea was a good one, a very good although small one at that time. My partner and I had nothing to loose at this point, only our time and I had spent quite a bit of that time getting us a meeting with Amena, which much later got bought out by Orange. The meeting was in one of the most famous buildings in Barcelona, Torres Mafre, down by the beach area of Barcelonetta. The same location we originally decided to try to start a business between us.

Leading up to the meeting I was pretty sure that my mind was far more on this idea than my partners and besides, all the actual idea's and their development up until now had come from me and not from my partner. For this latest idea I had spent several hours comparing pricing plans of all the other providers for individuals and even companies so that I had an idea what to expect from this meeting. For this business idea I was highly motivated and had done my research. Maybe as it was my idea my partner had not spent himself too much, or perhaps his mind was still on other ideas of his own.

Here in lies the first problem with partnerships, it's hard to quantify and monitor how much time and effort each partner puts in. Clearly if you feel you are spending far more hours working than your partner, and it is actually work, even at this stage, then there are grounds for some potential ill feelings. In my case I did not have a wife or even a girlfriend and so I was free to invest more time in the business idea than my partner and I certainly felt I was doing that.

In any case, for better or worse I kept all these thoughts to myself for the time being and ignored the advice of a friend, the very same friend who generally gives me no support for my ideas, remember him? That's two mentions he's got so far, how pleased he will be. It will be now harder to get him to endorse my book on the back, blast it. Anyway, his advice was that you should set up an official document with your expectations of the partnership and of your partners. For example, you expect a partner to work five or six days a week and eight hours a day. You expect no profit to be taken out of the company for the first year, things like that.

I did not do any of this, although I appreciated his input. The reason I didn't do it was more to avoid bad feelings and why bother when it would be impossible to monitor at this stage anyway. Another and more important reason, was, how would this document be enforced, so what if he was not working as hard as me, what could I do about it? Yes I could speak to him about it, and highlight the document, but I could also speak to him about it without this document. Anyway, it is a useful document to have and I would consider it in any future partnership, but at that time I just went with the flow.

So should you go it alone or do it together with a partner? I'll give you my experience here during this book, but you're situation could be quite different. What may not be different is that any relationship between two or even more people can be something quite difficult. If a marriage or a family relationship, or even a simple friendship with people you have known for years can be difficult, imagine the same intensity with someone you don't really know that well at all. All relationships have their twists.

In my particular case I guess I should have seen the signs way earlier than I did and one such sign showed its head leading up to the first big meeting with the potential provider, Amena. I had done my homework on the types of phones people liked to use, which back then was really just a case of which particular Nokia model you wanted. And as I mentioned I'd also studied the price of the various plans available and had an idea of the discounts we would need to be able make the whole thing work.

I also had the notion of presenting the idea to the provider as a chance for them to gain access to some smart MBA students who would no doubt end up in quite high positions in many companies around Spain and around the world. I thought this would be interesting for Amena as this may help them with future sales into larger Spanish companies. However, this had little impact, the sales person we met was not so far sighted as to see the future benefits of the association with these type of customers, he was just interested in the estimated monthly spend of our account.

Around this time my partner and his wife were busy moving their belongings from the UK and had taken several trips back and forth. My partner's wife had worked for Cadburys and he seemed quite proud of her achievements there. As she had good experience in power point and making presentations he himself had got her to do some of ours and asked me if I minded.

I was not actually that keen on the idea to be honest and did not see our power point slides as being so important for this meeting. There was also the fact that he had told me he did not want to go into business with his wife, as it would be too much time together being at home and at the office, and I certainly did not want another partner at this stage, especially as the one I had had up until now contributed not much if I am honest. However, I did not want to cause a problem, so I said nothing and let her do it. In the end I can't now recall how many, if any, of her slides we used to be honest.

In any case, the meeting with Amena, which just the two of us attended, went very well, better than we could have hoped for. They liked my idea and were keen to work with us. They even gave us some pricing and discount details that were very if not extremely encouraging. The problem I mention came when a few days later my partner said something along these lines:

"You know my wife put in quite a lot of effort into that presentation for us, she was up all that night on it." he said, to which I said something like,

"Oh, yes, it looked great, she did a good job."

But he had not finished yet and went on to say,

"Well I've not mentioned it to her, but what I was going to suggest was that maybe we should give her a share in the business for the effort she has put in. I don't know how you feel, but maybe 10 or 15% of each of our shares to show the appreciation for her effort." he said.

I was honestly quite dumb struck at that point. We were just about to officially form a company by then and so he was quite serious about actually including her in the official ownership of the company, just for a power point presentation, something I did not really even want her to do and nothing that made any difference to us getting somewhere with Amena at the meeting I had arranged. Yes I was quite horrified at what he was proposing. My response was something along the lines of,

"Well I understand and appreciate her effort of the few hours she put into this presentation. If you want to, well we can pay her a few hundred euros or something if you think that's right. However, not to argue, but I've put literally hundreds of hours in these months into this idea and I'm not so keen to give away a percentage of the company to someone just for a few hours." I said.

This was said it as politely as possible and he accepted and agreed and that was the end of it. However, it left a bad taste n my mouth. Imagine having an equal partner and then that partner's wife comes on board, taking from your 50% stake and all of a sudden they then have legal control of the company and now have two voices against your one.

In a similar situation I would never have proposed what he had and I would never have even expected my wife to charge for helping her husband in his new venture, which at that time was not even up and running. As they say, there is nothing as crazy as people.

So if you do enter into a partnership, it is a good idea to have things clear to start with. Things that you may have thought were clear already, just from common sense, may not be so clear to the other person. We all see things quite differently and as I found later on, we all see ourselves quite differently also.

My experience with a partner was one of the worst experiences of my life and this was a privately and well-educated, polite, sociable guy I had become partners with. We will see more later in the book about how this all turned out, but even though it did turn out terribly, and I mean terribly, I would like to think I still have an open mind and would still consider another venture with another partner.

This is perhaps foolish and maybe I am a glutton for punishment, but I try to see the best in people, although there are those that would argue with that I'm sure. Maybe my vision is tainted, but of course, to have a successful partnership is certainly possible and there are many examples out there. Just as you got divorced once, does not mean the next marriage will also end in divorce, does it? I hope never to find out......

People can say that there are certain characteristics that partners in order to combine well and maybe opposites do work, but to be honest, I would not read too much into this. If I were you I would just read as much as you can into the person and how they operate in all aspects of their lives. How do the treat people, especially how do they treat people when things don't go their way, that is when you really see the character of a person, when things are against them.

No one is perfect of course and we all lose our temper, but if this happens all too often, or the degree of temper loss is something you are ill at ease with, then this is not the partner for you. Naturally it is hard to see all these things before you enter into business with someone, it's not like you will have a business-dating period where only foreplay is permitted.

There will generally be one person who is more dominant on a daily basis than the other and that person may well then feel in charge or at least more in control. However, the other person will, as we all do, have their limits and may come a time when they have had enough and they will try to resist being controlled by the other. There are so many possible combinations and ways in which problems occur that we cannot possibly look at too many of them here, I will simply focus on my experiences and hope they give you some insight into the difficulties of partnerships, but please do use your own experiences with any relationships you have had, work or otherwise, to guide you also. People are people....

The Positive "Yes" Partner

I wont spoil the ending by continuing any further at the moment with my first partnership, but instead we will go back to my next partnership in Colombia, the one where we were to import westfield kit cars.

My partner for this business I would call a "yes partner". You maybe know this persona as a very positive person, someone whom in theory is great to be around. They never say no and they claim they can get just about anything done, anything is possible to this person and they tell you it can and will be done. Maybe there are people who do this that actually can fulfill what they say, but I have yet to meet any of these people.

My experience here was with a Colombian guy whom I had befriended after having met several times. Now there are certainly some cultural differences between a typical English and a typical Colombian. Not a big deal of course, but I am a person that if I say something then I tend to have a reason for saying it and I tend to follow through with what I have said. If I cant follow through then I would generally give notice and explain why, that's pretty much what I would and maybe you would expect and those are the sort of qualities I like and appreciate. These qualities are not to be found everywhere though and I guess so far I had tended to ignore the lack of these qualities with my friend, as this was a different culture.

In Colombia if you are perhaps meeting a girl for dinner at 8:00 pm and at 8:10 pm they have not show up, you may call them and ask where they are. If you get the answer back that they are in a taxi and just 5 minutes away, that generally means they have just got out of the shower. I have been with many a Colombian friend and the amount of small lies they tell is incredible. Rather than just telling the truth and risking the other person getting annoyed, they rather lie and prevent them getting too annoyed, only for them to be even more annoyed later when the truth arrives.

Anyway, to talk too much about Colombia would be a book in itself and business in Colombia is another world and its not one I want to be involved in again to be quite honest. As I mentioned before, if most, and I mean most men think being unfaithful is nothing to be guilty about, then I would rather not be in business with these type of people. It's a shame for the honest and hard working Colombians that cant get on in the world due to the dishonesty and corruption that is rife in their country, but well....

Getting back to the point, I had a few business ideas that I had discussed with my friend and he himself had several business ideas also. If you remember, this is Henry who always had a headful of business ideas. At that time I had a lot of time on my hands and for me it was more of a hobby as I did not see it turning into anything big to be honest.

If you remember the kit car business I have briefly explained, the two key things for this business were getting the cars approved in Colombia and getting customers for them, the latter of which is always key in any business of course. Getting approval meant getting the engine gas emission levels approved for road use. This was not as easy as it should be as nowhere in Colombia could they test said gas emission levels.

Now my business partner, being a yes person or what you would call a very positive person, assured me both of these key points he had under control before I even paid the deposits on the first and last two cars we ordered. First of all he had insisted that just amongst his friends and contacts he could sell several of these cars, he was convinced of it, and being so positive a person, he convinced me too. As for the technical side of getting approval in this market place, he also had another friend in the government department who could get us this approval for us, again, no problem at all and again, I believed him.

Great I thought; what could possibly go wrong? This person seemed to have friends in every area you could imagine and could solve any problem you could come up with. I had no reason to doubt him, it was a new culture and a new place to do business, hence I decided to go ahead and opened a 50 / 50 company with him. I went to see the UK manufacturer and arranged everything so we could purchase two of these products and export them from the UK and send them off to Bogota.

My role really was supposed to be just to handle the provider and the exportation. The rest, i.e. the importation to Colombia, technical acceptance and sales were for my partner to handle. As the products had to be manufactured, we had to pay a deposit for them and then a few months later we would pay the balance, when they were ready for export. It naturally made sense, that I would make the first payment to get the order rolling as I had a bank account in the UK.

Now I said we were 50 / 50 and that to my mind or anyone's mind I believe, means that we each invest 50% and dedicate a similar amount of time and effort. However, this as we have already discussed, is never clear-cut and it never will be unless you are both in an office 8am to 6pm each day.

Here the signs that there may be problems ahead also came early, but were also just as foolishly ignored. The cars were now being made and hence, from my point of view they can now be offered for sale, but all of a sudden the supposed customers my partner had were now nowhere to be seen. We were going to be able to sell six or seven of these no problem he had said, but now after only a month or two, it seemed we did not actually have a customer for even one of the cars.

This only got worse when the cars were actually ready and the time came to pay the rest of the 70,000 $US for them. My trustworthy and positive partner had no money, yes neither his 50% nor even 1% did he have to pay for these cars. I was, not for the first time in my business partnerships, quite amazed. He offered to pay me interest though on the money that he now owed me, this money would come from the sale of the cars that he had been so sure we would sell.

The reality is that when my partner said he had customers lined up, he really meant he knew one or two rich kids whom he thought would buy the cars. He had at best sent them a photo or two and they had possibly said the cars look great and with that, coupled with the amount of money they had, my "yes and positive" partner took it upon himself to be so positive as to tell me he could sell the cars no problem.

What happened to the rich kids in the end, why could he not sell the cars to them? Well, one of them ended up falling out of a quite high up window, maybe pushed, maybe off his head on drugs, who knows. There were apparently bucket loads of cash found in his apartment, so we can only guess the source of his income. And with that, there also fell out the window my partner's client base for our cars.

Naturally, as in any partnership, I have to accept part of the blame. I foolishly believed this guy's promises without perhaps insisting on meeting these customers, although in this case I think its just as well I avoided any such meeting. However, at the risk of being negative, and these days everyone seems to down on negative people, I should really have doubted everything he said. Still, if you doubt everything your friends or business partners say, then its a pretty poor relationship you have right there.

These days, there are so many of those books out there, you know the ones I mean. Those books that tell you that all you need to do is be positive and even just thinking positively will make great things happen. If you have even the slightest negative thought, the doors will virtually close on their own to all things in your life. I have friends who actually believe this and yet some of them are not successful at all, so I just wonder, well maybe its best not to wonder and just let them get on with it.

Now I certainly hope this book, which is simply trying to get you out there and give it a go, is not like those books. I am not telling you that you definitely will succeed and that you will all be multi millionaires, and less so just because you think you will be. What I would tell you is that you as a person will be better for the experience. I certainly wont say the word richer for the experience, as I don't want any confusion. Of course you should not go into an important business meeting with a face like death warmed up on a stove, that's just common sense. However, I'd rather go in there well prepared and knowing how to react to various outcomes than simply be positive and not knowing much about anything.

With my own experiences in business, I had become what many people would consider to be quite cynical. Other people, especially in my new cultural surroundings of Colombia, would find me even quite negative. However, we all see ourselves differently than others do, this is another reason why partnerships can be so hard.

Naturally when people have let you down, your trust in people decreases doesn't it? If your ex husband had cheated on you several times and then maybe your next husband had done the same thing, its common place that this wife will now feel all men are cheaters. In her heart she may want to believe this is not the case and her common sense tells her this is not the case, but it is certainly natural and I think understandable that she will doubt the men in her following relationships.

Does this make her a negative person? Well, I'd say its now normal that she may take longer than usual to build up trust. I also think its right that the men in her life should understand and even sympathize with her.

Back to business; what lesson can you and I learn here? I hate to say it, but at least you should have it in the back of your mind; if something seems to good to be true, it probably is to good to be true. In the excellent film, Ronin, with an amazing driving scene in it, Robert De Niro's CIA character, Sam, said,

"Whenever there is any doubt, there is no doubt."

Obviously we are taking things to the extreme here, and there will always be exceptions to any rule, but at the very least be on your guard. I was not on my guard and I should have doubted my "yes partner" from the start and that way I perhaps would not have had to doubt him so much at the end.

We remained friends though and in the very end, the very very end, things worked out in some way or another and I certainly could have been in a much worse position. My partner proved himself, apart from being a yes partner, to be a decent human being, although slightly dishonest having said that. You also must accept that we are none of us perfect and none of us are 100% honest all of the time, even with ourselves.

What could and should I have done differently? Well I could have focused on these two same elements of the business, which were fundamental. The first was the ability to get the car imported into the country. I should have requested a meeting with this supposed friend of my partner and got quite clear what was needed to get this assembled kit car, a recreation of a Lotus 7, into the country and registered on the roads. I should not have been swept along in the local mentality that anything is possible here if you pay the right person the right amount.

If I had been more thorough, something that I can admit is one of my character flaws, then I would have found out to get the car out of the expensive customs retention area, the engine would need to be passed for emissions by the local authorities. Having understood this and the irony that the country did not actually have a facility to test detailed emissions information, then I would have been far more cautious before investing my money.

The only final way around this problem was to show that the exact engine used in the cars we were importing was an engine in another model of Ford car that was already used in Colombia and one that had the US regulatory certificated from California, which would also be accepted in the country in Colombia. I wont go into details, but its possible the engine in question was not perhaps exactly the same as the one used in the other Ford car, but it was certainly close enough and it was not going to do any harm to anyone having a few more or less particles of carbon from these two cars.

The other major factor was my partner's ability to sell the cars and his contacts. I should have done my own research and not relied on his positive attitude that we would sell six or seven with no problem at all, especially when he did not even know the final price of the car with all the import taxes and bribes you have to pay to get things through the customs in this country; what an embarrassment.

4. Making It Official

You have progressed and developed your idea, either alone, with a partner, or maybe even in a larger group. You're now ready to take the plunge, or as was in my case, tie the knot. There is only so far you can go without officially setting up a company.

Forming a Company

Now this will involve different steps in most places around the world. There are actually studies you can find showing the levels of bureaucracy in various countries, so that may be worth having a quick look at if you are flexible about where you can set up. I have personal experience of setting up about five companies in different countries, but in general they say the UK and the US are potentially the easiest places and you can literally buy a company right off the shelf; how easy is that?

These off the shelf companies already have a name and in addition all the legal side is set up for you too; all you have to do is pay and have your name instated as the sole owner, if you are going it alone that is. The company may not have the name you would have ideally chosen, in fact it certainly won't have, but does that matter? The actual company name does not need to be the same as the "trading name", which is that one you use in the day-to-day running of the company.

Lets say Henry wants to call his burger joint Henry's Horrid Burgers, but he buys a company off the shelf that is called JPM Stanley. No problem here, he simply additionally purchases and registers the trading name of Henry's Horrid Burgers under his official company name, JPM Stanley. He can also set up his website HenryHorrid.com, which is probably available, and also purchase that under his official company name.

Hence, the general public will see the name he wanted them to see, his trading name, but his providers and the government tax office will see his official name. Henry cares little about the latter elements in terms of his company name, so there is no problem as you can see with getting an off the shelf company. Any further changes to shareholders or capital involved can all be adjusted online later, or with a lawyer if need be.

I myself with my first partnership in Spain did not have this off the shelf option available, in fact setting up a company in Spain is a little more complex, but not frighteningly so by any means. There is the option to let a gestor / lawyer do everything for you and you simply pay them a quite sizeable fee. This is an option many none or bad Spanish speakers choose, but it was not the option that we chose, even though my Spanish was far from good.

In Spain you can go directly to the notaries office and they will have a lawyer there that will guide you. As a very rough guide, since all of this you can find on line, you have to search the government database for the name you choose, to make sure it is available. You have to state what your company objectives are, where this is a standard legal document, copied from one place to another, where you just add that you are going do; buy, sell, rent, and provide mobile phones contracts, in our case.

In Spain at that time, you also had to open a bank account in the company's name, even though the company did not legally exist at that time, but yes the banks do this. You had to deposit and get a statement showing you had 3000 euros in that account. There are a few taxes, a few charges, the cost to register your website if you want one and pretty much that's it. It can all be done in a couple of days and it's not that expensive.

We did all that without even intermediate Spanish, so as the book says, if I can you can, and you certainly can if you are setting up in your own country and your own language! Try to set up your company as economically as possible, since very soon there will come other perhaps unexpected costs and well really, at this stage, you just need the piece of paper.

Unless you are someone with quite a lot of experience then your initial company capital should be the minimum allowed, which was the 3000 euros in my case. Its unlikely anyone you speak to at this stage will be that interested in the companies set up capital, but now the company is registered you can now start to get some of the few government benefits.

Now anything you buy for your company can be bought in the company name by asking the seller to provide you with an invoice with the that name and the VAT registration number that came along with it. This means you can normally reclaim the sales tax VAT. Don't perhaps think you can go and buy an Aston Martin though and reclaim the 20% tax on it, the governments of most countries are not so generous. You generally have to prove that the purchase is for use in the company, and your image is not so important to the government so a 20% discount off an Aston is out of the question I'm afraid.

Different countries have slightly different rules, but in general they are similar. However, some countries certainly enforce them a little more strenuously than others. Spain and certainly South America can be more lax and the accountants there know what they can and can't get away with, whereas I'd say in the UK, you pretty much can't get away with anything, not until you get to a much more successful level. Then I imagine you can get away with quite a lot more, something you often read about in the papers.

Still, I don't imagine many of us will get to Apple and Google's level any time soon. These companies get an almost free ticket in terms of corporation tax due to various loopholes and moving their money around the world. Perhaps the various governments turn a blind eye due to the jobs and investment they bring.

I can understand this viewpoint and yes the overall benefit is probably no dissimilar to that which all the foreign car companies that came and stayed in the UK during the 80's received. After all, if you give a company grants to develop land or reduce their taxes, at the end of the day it's the same thing; its less money in the government's hands and more money in the company's hands.

However, if the government is not actually offering you this benefit and you are simply avoiding the tax by taking advantage of convoluted international tax law, then that is something else and I fully agree these companies should be made to pay their fair share of tax as they make enough money off us all without steeling from the governments on top of this.

I'm not here as your personal assessor in terms of detailing all the steps to follow to setting up your company. There is more than enough free information out there on the exact processes to set up companies and then you may get more help from your accountant, if you hire one. I am more just commenting on such things and hopefully making you see that none of them are that complicated and certainly not to be afraid of.

In that vein you should of course know that whatever capital you put in the bank to start your company, well that's money and you can still spend it. I mean it doesn't have to stay in the bank. You can go and buy your potentially "none tax paying" apple laptop with it, or use it to rent premises. It is your money, or rather your company's money to be precise. Just remember to ask for and keep receipts for everything, absolutely everything you use that money for. From bus tickets to taxi fairs, from Starbucks (that's another one isn't it?) to stationary, keep them all and where you can, get a bill in your company name.

A Place To Call Home

You have officially set up your company, but you don't necessarily have anywhere to do anything with it. Do you need an office, a shop front, a warehouse? I'd say you certainly don't, not until you are ready to look for customers and even then it depends on what you are offering to your customers.

A home office is generally the best way to start and any meetings you need to have with providers or the likes, they can be held at their premises or in hotel lobbies, which are usually very accommodating for this purpose. A local B&B is probably not going to inspire much confidence or be interested in you holding a meeting there, but the nice hotels with posh bars and cafes are ideal.

You need to keep your costs down as long as you can, this is more than likely your own money at the end of the day, and even if it were someone else's money, don't throw it away, as if your venture fails, they will never give you any more and may want what they have already given you back again.

For most businesses however, there will come a time when you feel confident enough in your idea's ability to make money that you will want to rent some premises. In some cases, like Henry's Burger bar, he has no business without his location; if you remember it was right between Burger King and MacDonalds. In his case he also needs quite a bit of time to ready his location and transform it from perhaps a hardware shop to a restaurant.

For food places like this, licenses are also needed and of course they can't be granted until you have the location, so yes, in some cases a location will be needed a.s.a.p. as will the investment to make that location suitable for use. Now depending on the style Henry may have chosen, I would certainly use a designer or builder who understands what you want. And I again would take into account costs.

There are some amazing interior designs out there that are more rustic or have a warehouse feel that are quick and easy and cheap. Why cover walls in plaster board if an already exposed brick will look just as good. An exposed ceiling with its air con tubes can look great too with the right lighting and that is much cheaper than covering it all up.

Unless your clientele are Porsche driving, Rolex wearing, Paul Smith socked and Gucci shoed, you need to be smart and maybe invest a little in getting the right architect or interior designer, in order to save you in building / decorating costs. Google will help you getting photos of industrial style interiors or just a search of cheap and elegant cafe design will bring you many options, far more than a builder will ever suggest.

If your business is not a restaurant, a shop, a garage or something along those lines, then the chances are you can wait a while longer to find premises. Let's take my cell phone business where it was clear at some point we would need a place to be able to meet our customers, explain, offer and hopefully provide our service.

Most cell phone companies used shops to do this, but in reality we could have used an office and perhaps should have used an office. Why? Well we were going to target a niche market of international students, and hence, we did not want to give our service to the man in the street. Literally we did not want locals coming in asking us to fix their phones or explain our product to them, as our product was simply not for them. In fact, we may have been in danger of damaging our relationship with our provider if we did provide our service to regular Spanish users, as then we would be competing with the local distributors!

However, before we ever looked at locations, at least in more than just a price finding mission, we were more interested in other aspects of the business. The simple aspects of our business were to acquire a competitive contract with a provider, who by the way did not care much about our premises, and be able to repackage and sell said service. In a nutshell that was it and its good to have a plain simple idea of what your idea is of course.

In order to be able to do this, we naturally needed to be able to bill our customers for their usage. This meant being able to take the billing information from the provider, recalculate it and send it to our customers. Quite simple right? Well yes, very simple for someone who has data base experience, which I did not have, but my partner did.

However, it would have been foolish of us to progress to the point of getting a location, paying the rent on it and then going after customers before ever seeing the format of the bills from our provider. What if the information they provided us with was in a format that we simply could not use, or that then we really needed to use a professional to do the billing and this would take several months to set up.

So the simple point here is that you should go through the early steps of your business as far as possible and get all IT systems, websites and other processes organized, before you move to the next stage and look for a location. Remember, your location is possibly going to be your largest monthly cost initially at least, at least until you start to hire a few staff.

Something I've always liked the idea of, but never actually found the right opportunity, is using a dual-purpose location. I mean by this that if your business is to make sandwiches and breakfasts to deliver to workers at their office buildings, starting at about 5am each morning and then finishing early in the afternoon, why not try to find a location with a kitchen that is only used in the afternoon and evening and share said kitchen.

Just throwing an example out there, but I worked as a glass collector in a nightclub many years ago; I could tell you some stories from that work experience. This nightclub, as many do, had a kitchen with all the facilities for preparing and cooking food. Naturally this kitchen would at best be used 3 or 4 times a week and only ever between the hours of 10pm and maybe 3am. I would imagine that if you were to offer the nightclub owner a commission or a reasonable fixed monthly rent, they would consider letting you use their kitchen each and every morning, as long as you left it clean and made sure all and any employees were responsible. Undoubtedly this would be cheaper than having a whole location to yourself and would be a good way to start up without spending too much initially.

In the case of my somewhat embarrassing importing kit car business, we never looked for premises, as they were not needed unless we were going to invest a fortune. We simply imported the cars and finally relied on other shop windows to sell them, which they didn't, but that's another story. I also had parking spaces to store the cars and used my home as an office, so there was no need to spend more on something that I already felt would loose me money.

In the more realistic case of our mobile phone business back in Barcelona, property prices were booming, as this was way before the economic crash, which hit Spain harder than many other countries, but perhaps Barcelona a little less hard than other parts of Spain. Hence, any premises we eventually chose would not be that cheap and for some unknown reason we did go for a small shop on a side street than an office. I would say we only had our shop contracted maybe five or six weeks before we started getting customers.

By this stage our partnership had, without any formal discussions, reached a point where each of us knew our responsibilities. Later I would discover that this responsibility split was perhaps not to the liking of my partner, but it seemed logical at the time. My partner was the only one theoretically capable of taking the data from our mobile provider and producing the invoices for our customers. This seemed to be quite a major task and it took a few weeks for him to do and so meanwhile I got on with making a website and our promotional material.

Now, I will fully admit that although I like the subject of design, I am no designer. However, our customers were fellow students, they were not Aston Martin customers and so I really did not think it was worth spending money on professionally designed promotional material or indeed a professional looking website, at least not at this early stage. I was pretty sure that not many students would turn down our offer just as our website was not designed by someone who ate up most of our budget.

Likewise with our flyers, which I had great fun in designing; why spend money we didn't have getting a professionally designed one? I even invented our company logo, which I think I always knew my partner was not so keen on, but there is no arguing with results. We gave out about three hundred flyers and got about two hundred customers, that's a little better than the normal terrible return that most flyer campaigns get. I felt sure people would come to us for our ease of use, customer service and friendliness, not to mention speaking English to these guys and girls, most of which did not speak Spanish.

I'm not so clever to play on phycology, but when you know some ex students are starting a business and you see some maybe poorly designed info, I think in a way it doesn't necessarily put you off, instead it gets you a sympathy vote. This sympathy vote is certainly not won when you have some cheesy flyer with the supposed perfect wording and perfect teethed models, which is just what we had for the following winter campaign.

When it had come to finding a location, cost was probably a larger consideration than location, but we tried to compromise. Despite this, there were several comments of how hard we were to find. Our little shop only had an area of about 35 meters squared, it was an ex clothes shop. Coincidently another popular business to set up, especially for females, are back street clothes shops. Sorry to say though they are also another huge percentage fail, but that does not mean you will. If that's your dream and you think you bring something different and can drag those customers in through your doors, then go for it.

Traffic Is Your Friend

As I said, an office would have worked fine because part of my role was to visit the business schools and get our name out there. We used direct marketing, i.e. giving flyers directly to the potential customers via the schools staff or even outside their business schools. Hence, with a map on the back of the flyer, they could come find us. Eventually I managed to get all the schools to provide our information to the students before they ever even arrived to Spain and so then the website became more important as a marketing tool than the printed flyers.

So in contrast to most businesses traffic to us was not actually our friend, because most passers by are not are target customer and we could not receive them as customers. Since a large part of our business was based on risk taking, risk that people pay their bills; we really went after the expensive business school market and not the general man on the street. The thinking was easy, these students had earned big money before doing their MBA and hence were used to spending and paying larger bills than the average person. I also had a good reputation with the schools so they would perhaps apply pressure if they decided not to pay.

This is quite the opposite approach to a location for a clothes shop or Mr. Henry's burger bar. I've seen so many clothes shops, in Barcelona especially, which are on back streets that are quieter than a church mouse that's just been told to make less noise by his fearsome father. Never have I seen more than one person in these shops at any one time and I have no idea how these businesses survive and in fact, I think most of them don't.

Actually, for those of you who are thinking about a clothes shop and the only rent you can afford is a quiet back street, I can tell you a new craze in Barcelona, which I did think of before it started, but adds to your costs of course. Hanging around a busier street, just off which leads the quieter street where the clothes shop is located, you will now find the odd confident flyer giver.

This guy or girl will look at you walking down the busier street, decide based upon your age and dress sense if you are a potential customer for their shop, and then give you a flyer and tell you about their discounts and then points you to where the side street shop is located. This is their only real way to get traffic to their shop and it seems to be working for them as I've seen various people take the flyers and make the detour to the shops in question.

Of course your Zara's and H&M's wont need to do this and they will pay huge rents to be on the streets and in the shopping centers where there is a huge pass by rate, but without a big loan or a wealthy investor, you simply wont be able to budget that sort of location. Hence you do indeed need to think about how you get people to your shop or to your restaurant if its out of the way.

If you recall, Henry was using the pass by trade from his competition, but he will also hence pay a high price for that location. If he was on a back street or out of town, where rents would be affordable, then he would need to think more outside the box to drum up business. An obvious one is to advertise, but that of course costs money. A less obvious one is to work on trying to get free newspaper reviews. Perhaps inviting some critics along and hopefully giving them something they like, which they will then shout from the rooftops.

If I recall, Richard Branson started Virgin as a record company and before he ever had any shops he simply advertised his records in a newspaper and sent them out mail order. So again, he avoided a costly location and maybe he even did this from home? Either way, it worked quite well judging by his lifestyle today. He also proves that there are some people, not that many, but some who can turn their hand to various businesses. After all, an airline is quite different to a record shop or a fizzy drinks or mobile phone company.

I'd like to think my mobile phone company was more innovative than his, but well, I won't split hairs. I didn't quite have his investment to go along with my idea, but I'm not too jealous. I always respect other peoples businesses but I never tend to get jealous. There are so many ways to make money out there and it is often just a case of getting out there, being determined and being a little bit lucky, or at least not being unlucky. And in well, maybe being a little bit smart can help too.

If on the other hand the critic does like your food, this could spell the end of your venture. If you only get one bad review maybe its not too bad, as long as you are getting other good reviews from normal people. Still, you will need those normal people to spread the word and most of us don't do this. In order to encourage people to do this, you can try to think of benefits for them to do so. If they liked your food so much that they themselves will want to come back, then you can simply offer them a discount if they then send or bring another customer with them.

This is something quite common and I'm sure you've seen it in many places, although not many clothes shops do it to be honest, but I don't see why it would not apply to them just as much as to a food location. Customer loyalty is always good and should be encouraged. With most companies, from Porsche to the Natwest Bank, those that spend more tend to get even better prices and priority access to new products etc.

One shop in Barcelona, where I perhaps spent too much money on various occasions, although always in their January sales, always tries to take customers email addresses. Then using their database on how much the customers spent and perhaps the time of year they spent it, they send out a text message inviting them to the shops presale events. They invite you to go and get first access to their sales the day before they begin. This is quite simple and effective marketing; they are giving priority access to those that they know spend most, hence maximizing their potential sales over this period.

What's in a Name?

You will no doubt find many articles written by many people and they will tell you they know a great deal about the human mind and our habits. These people will doubtless tell you how important your trade name should be and how it could make all the difference to your business.

I recall my first partner telling me his wife had studied a lot about this and that a name with any negativity in it would be a very bad thing and it would be almost impossible to become successful with such a name. I remember at the time thinking,

"What a load of twaddle."

However, in order to prevent any issues, I followed their advice when I came up with our business trade name. The name I wanted to use was a slight play on Spanish and English, which I thought was pretty clever, but they clearly did not share my sense of humor.

The name was "SinMobile.com". The word sin in Spanish means without and in English, well its something we all do, isn't it? I had checked the availability of the website domain and everything, but I didn't want to be a possible reason why our business failed so I dropped that name.

In the end we went with another name I came up with, as I and that name was "MobileHigh.com". You can see here the complete opposite approach. One name is indicating that you are without a mobile so come to us and we will help, with a bit of humor thrown in, as after all our customers were students, not pensioners. The other name, well yes it gave a positive image in your head upon hearing it, as if getting a mobile with us would make you high or put you on a high.

However, if you were looking for a mobile phone after having just arrived to a new country, would you really be that bothered about the company name? If you knew they spoke English and you did not speak Spanish the chances are you will head there regardless of whether the name has a negative tone or not, but what do I know.

My advice to you would be try to choose a name that is easy to say and hence easy to remember and do bear in mind the type of customer you are looking for. Yes you could use humor as I was, but only if you feel your customers share your sense of humor. However, don't get to hung up on the name too much. The first few times I heard of google, I could not recall the name at all or even what they did. They don't have an easy to remember name like "easysearch" or something, but they seem to have done all right so again, just use your common sense.

On another note the name Apple does not make you think about computers as much as IBM International Business Machine does, but in the end look who won that battle. A name will only take you so far, and that far is no where near as far as you need to go and you will need to do other far more important things very well in order to be successful, so don't stress your name too much. Suffice to say, don't be sexist, racist or use insulting language though; that would not be ideal!

5. Marketing Or Sales

You have officially set up your company, you've chosen the name, you have your location, even if that be your home office for now and so, what do you do now?

Staffing

Before we get to the interesting bits, you will know by now how much you can and can't do on your own. You know your own skills and those of your potential partners and hence you should know how many people you will need to employ to help you. If we look at Henry, he probably isn't a great chef and even if he was, he couldn't then serve tables at the same time. Hence Henry needs staff for his fast food joint.

We now enter other realms of what you can and cant do on your own. Would Henry know enough about the law and accounting to be able to hire people himself? On google you can find advice on everything and I am sure you can easily find a standard work contract for a restaurant employee, which will save you having to pay a lawyer or more likely an accountant to do it for you.

Likewise and following similar advice you can do your own accounting and payment slips etc. If you feel confident in this, then yes why not, especially if things are tight budget wise, maybe it will be a stage you go through where you try to do everything yourself, I know we did when we first started. However, at the same time I would certainly get a quote on how much it would cost to get an accountant / bookkeeper to help you a few hours a week. Getting the right individual person on just a part time basis could save you a lot of hassle and time, which could be better, used trying to get customers through your doors.

I'd guess what would take you yourself a full few days a month will probably take this one person two or three hours a month and the relative cost wont be so high, we are not talking about using KPMG at this point, sorry KPMG. The invoiced cost of this person is also tax deductible so it all goes against the cost of the business. This will start to give you a good idea if the business is going well, i.e. if it can pay its realistic costs and accounting is certainly a cost you want to have covered. Don't forget you will have to declare your annual results at some point anyway and your VAT maybe every three months.

In terms of other staff, well for Henry a cook, cleaners and waiting staff would seem logical. In general if you have people you know that can work for you, family even, that's a good and a bad thing. Its good in that you suppose you can trust them, you know them at least, and so you would hope they are not going to steal from you.

However, its also bad as if there are issues and maybe they don't work the way you would like them to, then it probably makes it harder to change that and when it comes to disciplining them, that could cause other problems for you far further a field than just at work.

The one thing that generally rings true is that you normally pay for what you get. Yes you can be frugal when you are starting a business, or at least I feel you should be, but if someone feels they are being taken advantage of, well that does not make for a happy work environment. It can also lead to green fingers and as in the case of Henry, when there is a lot of cash around, you do have to be careful.

Along these lines, I have owned and even ran a hotel and there I'd say that out of the twenty or so people that worked there, fifteen to my knowledge stole from me. Be that money, coffee, bedclothes or bread, they stole something. Those with access to the money and registration of guests were obviously the ones who had an easier time stealing money and making false invoices to hide their theft. Those in the kitchen, well you can imagine the sought of things they stole.

I'd like to say that I have never done anything like that in my life, but if I am honest then I cannot. The problem is when you work for a company and see all these nice things around you; I guess the temptation just grows and grows. You may start taking just a pen or a pad of paper home as they are always handy to have and they don't cost much, so who will miss them right? That is still theft whether you like it or not, its stealing and its wrong!

The worst thing is that from then on, its just a small leap to a pack of highlighters and maybe a calculator or a pack of batteries for your son's remote control car; those things are always running down. Once you get it in to your head that it is okay to take something, no matter how small, then its just a small case of step by step until you get used to and feel comfortable with the idea of taking pretty much anything that belongs to the company, at least something that you feel you can get away with. At the end of the day its just the companies and not someone else's so it's okay, isn't it? Well no, of course it's not.

Along the same lines, we have taking a sick day to wait in for a package or go to your child's school sports day. You are stealing eight hours of wages in reality, that's no different than stealing cash from the company's financial point of view. It's a slippery slope to start on and from my point of view its then quite hypocritical to try to bring up your children to be honest, when you are okay with doing these kind of things.

As I said, I'm no saint, but I do try to catch myself and no, I wouldn't even take a hotel towel now and I would criticize those that do. You can buy the thing for 9 or 10 $, is it really worth stealing? This book should not be turning into the bible by any means, but after my hotel experience I would try to encourage anyone to think twice before even stealing a pen, what's the point? Set a good example, sleep easy at night and have a clean conscience and then maybe you can hope people will treat you the same way. It is worth certainly saying something along these lines to your staff, it cant do any harm, that and installing cameras.

Back to it; do try to limit the number of staff initially and yes try to do things yourself, as long as customers don't suffer, as if they suffer then ultimately so does your business. If a member of staff gets sick, actually genuinely sick, then you will have to cover or find someone to do so, but you shouldn't have to worry about these things initially, you can trust to luck a little I'd say.

I'd rather have three very busy waiting staff than five very bored ones. I'll happily put up with them being run off their feet and giving them a bonus for their hard work, if that saves me employing further people, at least until I really know the business is going well, over the first couple months or so. Explaining the situation to your staff also makes sense so that they know this wont be the case forever as neither they nor your customers will put up with it.

When you have money coming in to cover these extra staff, well that's a different story and yes its nice to not have to be stressed out every time someone is sick or has a days holiday, which they are entitled to of course and these twenty or thirty days a year must be taken into account at some point.

There is a saying that's worth taking into account though and I am sure we have all been guilty of making it true,

"People's work tends to expand to fill their day."

If I have one office assistant and he or she is having to stay maybe ten or twenty minutes extra each day to finish their work, as there is simply too much work for them to do in the regular eight hours, as soon as I hire one other person, you would have logically thought that with these two people they would be finished very early in the afternoon and could theoretically go home early, but no. This is what the expanding work theory means. We generally allow the work we have to occupy our whole day, even if it actually doesn't need to. You will find these two people now still have enough work to occupy them all day long.

What Is Marketing And Do You Need It?

Anything that helps get word out about your product or service is one form or another of marketing. However, going to extremes, even though they say no publicity is bad publicity, I am sure our friend Henry would disagree if a local newspaper reported having seen a rat running from his kitchen with a burger in its mouth. So not all publicity is always good publicity.

I have spent quite a good deal of time in sales during my life; I worked for one company in sales for about six years. However, when I started my first business, the cell phone business, I would say my main role there was still actually sales. When you have your own company and your partner is busy making data bases for billing your customers, then someone has to focus on how to get those customers to you.

If I were you I would not worry too much about the distinction between sales and marketing, just think of marketing as simply a device to indirectly help you get sales. Where as sales is simply someone directly trying to get you the same sales. It matters not if a business school or another author sees things another way, at the end of the day what you are interested in is getting sales, without that, you have no business, unless your business is a formula one team which does not need actual sales, but instead sponsorship for example, but you get my meaning.

I have long since known that you or me or Henry could have the best product known to man; a tablet that makes you invisible; a new material which repels all dirt; or even a time machine. Whatever it is you are offering, it is quite useless to your business unless people know that it exists. This is the first step; after this they may also need to trust it of course.

I'm sure there are many products that could be very useful to me; something to fold my shirts for example when it comes to packing a suit case. At the same time, if I don't know about the existence of such a product, then I will never buy it and possibly not many other people will either. Naturally, and as is the case with most products you could possibly think of, such a product does in fact exist, but then as its not in easy reach, maybe at my local supermarket, I still don't buy it. This is then another problem, your sales channel.

If you have designed an item to help you fold shirts in an instant, and I do know there are many such devices out there, then your main goal will be to get them into areas where they are easy to find. If you think about it, you may believe most people may buy these items when they buy the shirts, hence maybe try to get them into clothes shops. Or you may decide its better when people buy luggage or when they buy ironing boards. You will have to be inventive in your positioning of your product, but that's good fun too.

Depending on the initial investment available for your start up company, marketing will perhaps be something you feel you have to skimp on. Be careful here though. Yes you can try to spend less as you simply don't have it, as was my case with my leaflets and website come to that, but you do need customers, without them you have no business, in most cases.

In fact, when you are in the process of developing your idea, you should have in the back of your head, and right from the very start, how are you going to get word to your potential customers? If you are more technical and not able to think about this side too much, then a partner would certainly be a good idea that is more apt in this area. With my first phone company it was quite easy to get to the customers and that's partly why I started the business and partly why it was successful; my customers were all split up into nice large groups and they spent each day in the same buildings, i.e. their business schools.

I knew that in the first case a flyer hand out right outside these buildings would get me direct access to my potential customers. The flyers may have been unprofessionally designed, but the message was clear and the service was the best available, at least customer service.

The technical service did have its drawbacks in terms of coverage, but well, there is no perfect business of course. The schools, or at least one of them that we stood outside, IESE business school in this case, was not happy with our standing there. In fact, the director of admissions came outside and told us to move, but by that stage we had given out most of our flyers so it mattered little.

We were on public property, i.e. the footpath, so there was little she could do, but I did not want an issue with the largest school we were trying to provide our service to, so we respectfully backed away from their premises. You will come up against certain barriers, far more stringent than a lady who feels she controls an entire university, but stay calm and live to fight another day.

Our friend Henry, with his clever physical positioning of his burger joint, needs less marketing. Having spent quite a lot acquiring his location next to the other Kings of the burger world, he has perhaps done enough to tempt their customers to come in and try his product. A few flyers or free mini samples might also help, but he should not need an expensive marketing campaign to get word out there; his sign should be enough to do that.

In your case, you probably wont be so lucky; you probably will need to do some form of marketing. Direct marketing is usually most effective if it is possible. This is where you target your marketing activities at your specific customer type, rather than just general advertising. When we handed out our flyers to the students of IESE there was no more direct marketing than that. However, if we had simply placed an advert in a local ex-patriot magazine, of which there are a few in Barcelona, then that would not have been direct but more general marketing; it also would have been quite expensive.

I do actually remember later placing an advert in an Easy Jet in flight magazine, mainly as their sales person convinced me it would lead to customers from the ex pat community, just as I am now trying to convince you against such things. In my mind, where else, I knew it wouldn't really be worth it and, in the end my mind was proved right. I got maybe two requests for information from the advert that cost far more than five or ten customers bring me in profit during the whole year. Yes, the sales person then tried to convince me to give it time, it was their job of course, but no, I was a direct marketing kind of guy.

When you look at how to get word out there regarding your business, try to brain storm as much as possible and if you can, do this with other people. There is rarely any harm trying new things that mainly just cost a bit of your time, rather than money.

I recall a business very much along the lines of Craig's List having started in Barcelona. I even met the founder of this business at a small gathering at the house of someone who worked for Private, one of the largest porn companies around. Soundsglamorous doesn't it? Well it really wasn't.

Anyway, this guy had created his database style website, and that was effectively his business, a database for his customers to use to advertise their things or services on. As I said, pretty much a direct copy of Craig's List if we are honest, and this again goes to show you don't need to be a huge ideas person or have that one special amazing idea; you can pretty much copy someone else's idea if all else fails.

This guy, from Puerto Rico I believe, he had a very direct and relatively cheap way to get word out there about his website. He printed hundreds, and probably thousands of bookmarks. I guess back then, way before the ipad and kindle, people still read books and so a free bookmark was happily picked up wherever he left them. He tended to leave them in Irish Pubs and generally anywhere that ex pats tended to hand out.

In the end his website was not only used by English speakers, but that was the initial market he was aiming for. No big and expensive advertising campaign for him, just bookmarks and a bit of boot leather. In terms of names, his was another one I could simply not remember, it took me probably a year and ten visits to the website for it to sink in, it was Loquo.com, I think; you see what I mean!

I personally would not recommend a difficult to remember name, but maybe I just have a bad memory as several years later there was a Loquo website for just about every city in Spain and then all over Europe. In the small print I think I saw the company then belonged to Ebay. So I imagine and hope he did quite well for himself, all from walking around and working his idea as hard as he could. In fact, thinking about it, I believe his site was free to use, so I guess only advertisers would have provided him revenue. It certainly became a popular place to look for a room to rent, and several other things to rent in the XXX section, not that I ever went there of course.

To Make Money or Not?

It seems obvious doesn't it? Of course you are starting a business to make money, otherwise you may as well keep working for someone else and have him or her pay you. However, depending on the type of business you are setting up, you may have to wait anywhere between weeks and years to make money. And I'm not just talking about breaking even either.

Henry would no doubt hope to receive some actual money from his very first customer, for his first burger sold, which makes perfect sense. Naturally he has spent some money on decorating, preparing and equipping a kitchen. On top of this he has his high monthly rent, in such a prized location, and staffing costs etc.

So yes Henry will hopefully receive some immediate income, but it may still take a few weeks before he covers his monthly outgoings. Even that being the case, I'd say he would be quite happy if after just one month his takings are higher than his outgoings. Although even if this is the case, he still has a way to go before he can say he has even broke even, as he has to pay back his capital expenditure on his establishment. This could take anywhere from six months to maybe two years, depending on how much he takes out of the business as profit for himself and what terms he has set for the repayment of his or someone's loan to the company for said expenditure.

In my own case and with my first business, we were also quite happy that after literally just one month we were in profit and could even pay ourselves a salary. For our business, the main investment was a deposit we had to pay to our mobile phone service provider, Amena. However, in theory this money was always ours and would always be refunded as long as we paid our bills and fulfilled our commitments, so it wasn't really an investment in the strict sense of the word.

On top of this, for each phone line we contracted, and we were pretty much forced to contract about three hundred of them to start with in order to get the pricing plan we wanted, we also received a free mobile phone. Yes, back in the day, before young people started spending a months salary on a cell phone, the cell phone companies generally gave you a free hand set as long as you signed up for a period of at least a year if not eighteen months, and spent a set minimum each month.

Amongst these three hundred phones we got a mix of mostly Nokia but also Sony and Motorola. There was a Nokia phone I was crazy about back then, I think it was the 7250i. At my previous job I had used an 8910i that I thought was great at the time and later I had a small Sony, which had a little wheel at the side of it and a flip down part to protect the keyboard. It was tiny and I still have it today somewhere, fifteen years later. Anyway, we got some of my favorite phones, the 7250i, of which I took one of course, like a kid with a new toy, and my partner also took one.

All these phones were free! I think the average value of the phones we had, back then in about the year 2002, was about 130 euros. So our provider happily gave us 300 x 130 = 39,000 euros worth of phones. In return, we had to use 300 phone lines and pay a minimum bill in each one of about 15 euros a month, and that was for a period of 18 months.

Now for the astute amongst you and even just those that can multiply, you will see that our provider, which later became Orange i.e. French Telecom, on the one hand was giving us handsets worth 39k euros and only asking us to spend during 18 months a total of 27k euros. Seems crazy doesn't it, well this is why I was so happy after the first meeting with them and this is why I was very annoyed my partner expected me to give up a share of this company to his wife for a few hours work.

This to me was better than selling water or even fresh air, considering I also got my free toy. There was one condition attached though, theoretically we were only lent these phones; we had to give them back at the end. However, we were told that no one ever gave them back and no one ever went and asked for them back.

First lesson, well one of them at least; get it in writing. As our customers would generally leave the country after their MBA or Masters course, they would no doubt be leaving with the phone they acquired from us and hence, we would find it very hard to get the phones back. This being the case, we requested a written document from Amena that stated that they would in our case not claim the phones back at the end of 18 months. I don't know how we got this, as no other customer got it, but we did!

Naturally with tri-band phones still not being so widespread, we had to provide our customers with phones, but we were not as generous as our provider was to us. We had no intention of giving these phones away for free, no matter (within reason) how much anyone spent with us. So although we maybe did not manage to charge the actual value of the phone, an average 130 euros to our customers, we did probably charge an average 80 or even 90 euros.

You can see in the next immediate section how this worked out for us, but I wanted to quickly mention the mobile phone application "whatsapp". I'm not just mentioning it as it eventually became a huge application for my customers and indeed for millions in the cell phone industry, especially outside the USA, where they are still a little behind the times and use regular text messages.

No, I mention whatsapp as this company is a good example of an idea that did not initially intend to, and even to this day perhaps, make money directly from its customers. If you use their application you will still possibly be using it for free. A few years ago there was a message upon downloading the app that it would be free for 1 year and then they would be charging 99p for its continued use after that point, per year that is.

Most people ignored this message of potential cost and downloaded the application anyway, or would be simply happy to eventually spend such a miniscule amount for a product if they found they were using it, and certainly in Europe and beyond, people do indeed use it. So this raises the important question, why would anyone want to start a business that is not going to make money?

Well I would say first of all that's really not the case here at all. In the back of their minds, those that started the company were always intending to charge for their service. Its just that they wanted to wait until they had you hooked on it, until it was an intrinsic part of your life and that you could not do without it. At that point you would be happy to pay the 99p or even maybe 999p per year to use it.

When they reached a worldwide customer base of several hundred million, well that's quite a few 99 pences we are talking about, and that's quite a yearly revenue. In the end though and before they ever got to the point of charging you, they were actually bought out by an even larger company, but lets not go into it too much and just look at the simplified model they chose.

They made their product free to their customers in order to attract customers in a difficult market place. Back then the market place was dominated by BBM (blackberry messenger), Microsoft MSN, simple text messages and other products for certain markets such as Line. I'll leave you to figure out, if you are interested, the advantages and disadvantages to each of these, but I will say that if Blackberry had not kept their excellent BBM product tied to their own devices for so long and saw what their competition in "Whatsapp" was trying to do, maybe they would have saved themselves and been able to fight back against Apple's iPhone.

Now for most of us when we start a business we don't really have the option to work for several months, never mind several years, without any sales revenue. However, the guys who started this business and all the programmers who developed their app are not working for nothing, I can assure you. What they did was to look for investors, patient investors, who were willing to wait for their return on investment and in the end I'd say they got a great return!

The same applies to Tesla these days and even Amazon, who started out and indeed kept going for a long time with investors paying for everything and receiving very little in return, apart from hope. Amazon was perhaps the largest retailer in the world that was still not in profit. However, their idea was so strong and it was so clear it would come into profit one day that they just ploughed on.

If your idea requires a lot of investment and whether you intend to charge or not, it will be harder to get off the ground. I would never say don't go for it as there are Angel Investors out there that you can find on Google and if your idea is good enough and well enough presented, you will find someone to invest in it, I am sure!

Conditioning Your Conditions

The most difficult condition for my partner and I, and really the only condition put on us by Amena, out provider, was the minimum spend per month per phone line. Cleary our provider was not simply going to give us three hundred free phones and have the lines with no use and hence receive no revenue from them. Actually at the time there was a company that did just that, they took several hundred new phones for free and basically ran away with them all and never spent a penny. I think this happened to Movistar in Madrid.

Now whether you are applying for a new job, a new contract, or a marriage, there are always conditions, quite long contracts in some cases with conditions most of us don't even read. These conditions are put there to protect one side or the other, and sometimes even both sides. However, some of these conditions maybe unfair and you have the right to negotiate them, or try to.

Naturally when you are starting up on your own and you are dealing with a provider that has existed for many years and has many customers, they don't need you as much as you need them. Hence, negotiating with them may be quite difficult, but there is no harm in trying. Their sales person will normally have some sales targets for each quarter and if they have not met them, then your enterprise may be just what they need and hence a bit of flexibility may come into play.

As they say, "If you don't ask, you don't get." and there is generally little to loose if you do ask; they can only say no. These conditions may strangle your business and be part of the reason why you don't get off the ground, so it's worth trying to negotiate them. It's certainly worth trying to find other providers and trying to play one provider off another in order to limit or hopefully eliminate certain conditions.

In our case, the main condition that had us worried was the minimum spend on each phone line. We couldn't just take a line each time we signed up a new customer; our provider wanted us to take 300 new lines all at once, that was our minimum to be of interest to them lets say. We did at least get ourselves in a position where we took these lines in blocks over a few months, so the clock was not ticking from day one. We could activate fifty lines one week and another fifty a week later and so forth.

We only managed to get 180 customers at our first attempt, during the first intake of students in August - October 2002. This meant that the minimum spend would have taken away quite a large chunk of our profits. It would have meant us having a monthly wastage of the other 120 lines at 15 euros each, which would have been 1800 euros a month down the drain. That for us, and at that time, was the kind of salary we would have initially been happy to draw, so it was worthwhile negotiating, and negotiate we did.

As we were really the first company trying to set up a business of this kind, certainly in Spain, there was a certain amount of curiosity with our provider and hence, maybe a certain amount of flexibility other companies would not have received. We were what are commonly referred to today as a Virtual Provider, albeit in a slightly grey area as our name did not appear on the screen of the phone when you made a call.

We were in reality a cross between a reseller and a virtual provider lets say, but it matters not. There were only three operators in Spain at this time, Amena (later Orange), Vodafone, and Movistar, who were part of Telefonica, which was the same as British Telecom and French Telecom, i.e. the original monopoly that controlled all land lines in their respective countries.

In the UK I beleive the market was already opening up at that time. Virgin mobile was still a way off, but regulators were starting to open the doors to competition and hence were forcing the main operators to rent their antennas and services to other providers.

Anyway, we tried and tried and pleaded and pleaded and maybe even threatened to not do the business at all, unless we could get the minimum spend on each line, spread across all the lines. Meaning we were happy to say that on average all the 300 lines would have a spend of 15 euros, so our minimum bill a month would be guaranteed minimum 4500 euros a month, but that there could be within that total some lines that did not actually spend anything, as long as there were other lines that of course spent far more.

This point was eventually agreed; I think they were sick of us by then and just wanted to move forward. It was an important victory, but if our business totally failed, we would still have a risk of 4,500 euros a month, that's 54,000 euros a year. On top of this, our provider was not stupid, they rarely are, and they requested us to pay deposits of about 60,000 euros to cover their risk, especially in relation to the 300 handsets they were giving us for free.

So my partner and I had invested, albeit a relatively well protected investment, of 30,000 euros each. On top of this a very moderate investment in two computers, a laser printer and the tiny shop we rented. Oh, in this shop the previous occupants had left a huge and very heavy safe. So guess where we kept the excess mobile phones that we did not need to sell to customers.

Actually, these mobile phones eventually became a good source of additional revenue. On the black market these phones were indeed worth the 130 euros, or more in some cases, that our provider valued them at. We had 120 left of them over after selling the other 180 to our customers, so that was indeed a very good deal. As I said, at that time, I'd rather have had that business than the one of selling bottled water. Walking down some of Barcelona's darker alleyways, it was not hard to find places where foreigners could make international phone calls and these slightly dodgy locations also sold unlocked cell phones.

They paid cash and wanted no invoice, so it was a nice side revenue to our business. Naturally we declared everything as we did not want any problems with the taxman. Even still, it really is true what they say, cash is king. Credit is a terrible thing in business, try to avoid at all costs giving credit and people owing you money, cash up front, even at a discount, is the best way to be.

"One in the hand is worth two in the bush."

6. Success or Failure?

How do you judge your success or how long before you actually decide your venture has failed? I'm no expert but I have seen quite a few people keep on and on, flogging a dead horse basically, and not knowing when to give up. At the same time I've also seen some people start to see the money come in and relax, rest of their laurels and that can lead to its own problems.

Failing

Lets get failure out of the way first then. I was lucky in my first business, but if you read the last chapter then you will see it would have been very hard for me to fail in reality. The financial side was so stacked in our favor that we would have had to get almost no customers at all in order to fail, but of course, that was also possible I guess.

However, the business idea was so well developed and there was a clear need of which I had personal experience, something that really helps. I believe I had a natural affinity with my customers and because of my experience of having recently done what they were now going to do, people trusted me and that's always a bonus when you are offering a product. Besides all this, we had no direct competition; it was a true niche market.

While I was starting and running that business, I met several other people setting up their businesses. It's a bit like taking your children to school; you're bound to meet other parents aren't you. I became friends with another pair of Ex-MBA students who had gone down a similar route of looking for a product for their fellow students. Without being insulting, their product was a little less innovative, but was certainly something that was needed just the same.

Their business was providing housing to incoming students to their Business School, IESE. And then, in small part with my help, offering the same service to other schools too. At their school there was a big board or list if you like, where landlords could put up details of their properties for students who wanted to share and rent them. So these two ex IESE students basically contacted these landlords from this and offered to be their agents, taking care of supposedly everything. From advertising the properties, receiving the contacts from the students and showing the apartments. Then they would do the rental contracts and even take care of the maintenance of said apartments.

I don't know if they charged each side of, I have a feeling they did, but they were actually providing a service to both the landlord and the students, so I guess they were within their rights to do so. Soon they had some thirty apartments signed up and with an average of three or four bedrooms that was enough to accommodate over one hundred students. They were clearly going after the same customers as ourselves, a niche market that they were confident of attracting, as there were few if any companies offering this kind of dedicated service to students at the time.

As they could only provide for about one hundred students, where as we could basically attend any amount we wanted to, even passing the 300 initial lines we had to fulfill, we were in reality a help to them. When you arrive to a new country, and this is long before roaming and tri band phones remember, the first thing you need is a cell phone to be able to keep in touch and to call apartment advertisements. No one expects to arrive to a new country and in just twelve hours have a place to stay for the year, but they do expect and need a phone in this time.

Skipping a year or two, this apartment rental business had grown quite a lot, but also there had joined in quite a bit of competition to the student property rental market. Remember, it is often easier to copy an idea than to invent a new one. On top of this, when you are in a niche market, you are also maybe more vulnerable than if you weren't in a niche market. It only takes one of the larger providers to maybe open their doors to your niche customers and then your niche market is not so niche anymore.

In their case, this happened after probably three or four years. Apartment agencies or real estate agents basically, that had originally focused on selling and renting to Catalans, now saw that it would not be a big effort on their part to dedicate a little effort to foreigners. All they needed was one person in the office that spoke English and to get their property owners to understand that a student of thirty years old, paying about 50,000 euros for their course, was just as likely to pay their rent as anyone else, maybe even more so, as they did not depend on having a job during that time of study.

Another disadvantage of a niche market like ours was something that was originally an advantage, but one that could easily turn sour! The advantage I am talking about is having all your eggs, or in this case, most of your customers in one or two locations. This made our direct marketing, if you remember, a very easy job, it was just a one afternoon leaflet drop or later a visit to the schools and a kind word in the ear of an admissions advisor who could then send our information out to the soon to be arriving students.

The downside of this advantage though was that if you get a few difficult customers who feel your service is not as good as you think it is, or they feel tricked or mistreated, word spreads like wild fire around all the rest of your customers. In my case, I always tried to treat my customers with honesty and the best possible attention; this was something I had done in my previous employed role involved in sales. Certainly things can happen, but if you can foresee them or react quickly, then usually you can minimize most problems.

In the case of my friends apartment business it did not take long after their first customers left their contracted apartments after the twelve or eighteen months contracts came to an end, before the complaints against their company started surfacing. The most common complaint I recall was that this company was not refunding all or in some cases any of the deposits that the students had left in order to start the contracts. This deposit could have been a couple of thousand euros.

I am sure the company had their reasons and it was probably the landlords who saw the wear and tear of their apartments being too much for them to accept. In Spain it is the case that landlords unrealistically expect you to give them back the keys after even 4 or 5 years with not even a mark to be on the walls or floors etc.

My own experience of having rented a nice apartment and having paid a 6 months deposit was for the landlord to try to withhold about 3 months of that deposit when I left, in order to buy a new dishwasher, which I never even switched on, and a new fridge as it had a slight dent in the door. This bad experience is engraved in my memory forever. I had to contract a lawyer in order to get the landlord to be reasonable and accept that during the full five years I was living in the property, there would be normal wear and tear. I won the case, but still I lost more of my deposit than I would have done in another country lets say, but well, each country and each person has their peculiarities.

Well, dealing with so many foreigners who were not used to these peculiarities, lets say again, there were quite a few disagreements we heard about. I heard about a fair few of these disagreements as most of their customers were also our customers and I had quite a close relationship with my customers, considering it was a business I was running. Hence, they tended to tell me of their problems along these lines.

This situation soon put my company in a quite difficult situation as we were recommending my friends company's services and to be honest, I did not want to then be blamed for having done so. How could I keep recommending something when in the end the majority of the customers were not happy with it?

I initially defended and explained how Spanish landlords and contracts worked, but in the end I kept out of it and I gave our customers unbiased advice and sent them to three or four companies who now offered this type of service. One thing led to another however, and even with their own school trying to help and protect them, the word was out. Any new students arriving to even IESE were being warned by previous or current students not to use the services of this company. With this negative marketing effect, it did not take long before the company stopped working in this area altogether. Highlighting the disadvantage I mentioned above about having many eggs in very few baskets.

Out of interest, my friends first tried a name change and to put the company under different management, which maybe deflected attention and prolonged the company's existence for a while, but in the end they still failed. Well, maybe they didn't ... We will come back to them later when we talk about developing and keeping one step ahead.

I also made friends with another person, he actually rented a room from me at that same apartment where I paid such a large deposit and got slightly burnt in the end. He was and is a very nice guy, still friends to this day, but now more distant as he lives in Africa. I actually leant him money or in a way agreed for him to use my name and credit history in order to get a new car in Barcelona. Although this in the very end worked out, after the car was in fact put up for sale, then stolen, then recovered, then paid for by the insurance company etc, I would still not recommend lending money or your potential credit history to anyone, especially if you value your friendship.

This guy was a designer by profession and had worked with some guys in the USA in starting a business, which became quite successful, however now he was looking for something new and wanted to be in Barcelona, as many people did at that time. I saw several of his business ideas and he worked quite hard at them, but for a designer, there is so much competition out there.

I remember speaking several times with him while he rented a room from me before he then moved into his own flat / art studio. He had now started his own business in Barcelona, but there was no real money coming into his business that I could see, although each time there was the promise of something.

There was always a new contact that would offer a lucrative opportunity, but then it would take a while to come to fruition. Then by the time that one fell through there was now another opportunity that yet again seemed a sure thing. All these possibilities kept him and his business going for a while, maybe a couple of years even.

He was paying for a warehouse type location, not big and expensive, but still I'm sure it and other costs were biting a hole in his pocket. I felt very lucky with my business and based on my experience I had to say I thought he should close. He had tried for well over a year and had virtually no income and I think his brother who worked with him shared my feelings.

In the end, after maybe three supposed great opportunities all turning to dust, one after the other, he did close that business. However, then he started a T-shirt business. This idea had been done all too many times and every graphic designer in the world has at some point designed a T-shirt.

Sure, maybe a handful of them made money from it and those are perhaps the ones you see, but for each one of them, there are literally thousands that don't make money from it. A T-shirt design can be so subjective as to whether the public thinks its good or not and then there is the sales channeling, where and how do people buy them. The vast majority of us buy our clothes from a known retailer, either on the high street or on line.

In fact, now I recall that another designer friend, the one who did my second website and later did some flyers for me, he was also trying to start a T-shirt business. So in the whole world I only knew two graphic designers and they were both trying to start a T-shirt business; that speaks volumes. It will come as no surprise to you that neither of these businesses worked out.

Is there a conclusion to be drawn here? I certainly don't want to put people off the idea of starting a business, I'm writing this book with quite the opposite intention. Also I have said there is no such thing as a "bad idea" in business. However, I did say that in terms of that an idea goes through its development and can morph into something quite different than the original thought during this development process and well, in some cases it really needs to do so.

So yes you can sell T-shirts, but you would have to have a clear and workable plan and your products would need to be theoretically better, more interesting or cheaper than others already out there. This is something you can come up with, but one of the simplest ideas, although not the cheapest, would be to copy Henry's location approach.

Open a shop beside Zara, decorate it far more interestingly than Zara or have another way to drag the passing traffic in to your shop. Then it will come down to your actual product, although paying high rent to be there will mean your T-shirts will now perhaps be more expensive than you would have liked them to be, but if they are good enough, you could still get your customers.

Sticking there though, just as an example, at what point would you think, "that's enough, this isn't working"? People come in but they are not buying enough of my T-shirts to pay the rent, never mind the staff. This final decision of how long to stick at it may not depend on you of course, if you have investors, they may pull the plug long before you want them to. If you have a patient partner, husband or wife, or even parent, you may want to take them, their feelings or their money into account.

There are many factors that can make you call it a day, but I think it's important to think of these factors before you even start. I don't want to put you off starting, far from it, I just say that in your head maybe you should have a plan of expectations and stick to it. Its like going to a car auction, you know what car you want and how much you can pay for it. However, most novices, like I would be, get carried away in the emotion of it all and perhaps don't want to loose face and so they go over their pre-set limit and this can end in tears, especially if the car is not quite as mechanically or structurally sound as it appeared to be.

I also talked about using worse case scenarios. This isn't to be pessimistic, just to be pragmatic and it can actually encourage more than discourage. We can easily apply this to thinking about the business not working out and well, knowing what you will loose. In this thought process, you must put a time frame though and don't be tempted to extend it. There will always be hope, there will always be some new promise or possibility come along. On top of this, if there was no hope inside you then probably you would not have started the business in the first place, but hope will only get you so far. However, you must set and stick to your limits on time and investment.

Besides, just because you find yourself having to close this venture it does not mean you cannot start another. Add to this the experience you now have and the lessons you should have now learned. Plus perhaps the contacts you have made; this may all mean that the next time it could be easier!

Is It A Success?

Seems like an easy question to answer doesn't it, but it's not as easy as you may think. If your order book or bar or whatever you have started is full and your bank manager is welcoming you at each visit with open arms, then the chances are you have made a success of it yes. However, if this is not quite the case, but you still have receivables higher than outgoings, this does not necessarily mean it's a success, you cant quite retire yet.

While its better not to dream or get carried away too much when you are forming your business, you should at least have some basic numbers that tell you what kind of profit you would hope to make and by when. Breaking even is of course an important milestone in terms of your incomings and outgoings, without even considering the initial investment, but you are generally starting your own business to make your life better financially and so you need to go a lot further than having a "net" income of zero which is what this breakeven effectively is.

Its impossible to generalize here as each business is different and each person will finance it and do it differently and besides that, they will have slightly different expectations. However, you should take into account the stress a business brings you and your family apart from anything else. I would say it's not even good enough to just be in the same position and earning the same money as when you worked for a company, even though you are now your own boss, you should be aiming higher than that.

Remember, you wont now have sick pay, vacation pay, or a pension included, so all of this must be balanced against just your pride. When starting out, you need to set realistic goals and realistic time frames for each step, where getting to break even is certainly one of those steps. After this step will come the capital pay back, but most likely at the same time you will want to draw a salary yourself. While drawing this salary, and depending on how much this salary is, you can now give yourself a sizable pat on the back though and say your idea and business is now a success.

If your business is not quite so simple and is more a long term project, which maybe depends on getting people signed up to your website and access to some of their information, without actually charging them anything for example, well again, you must have set goals. You must decide initially whether after six months you should have 6,000 or 60,000 customers. Here, your customer database maybe replaces your cash income, but similar decisions need to be taken.

Should you have no other income, i.e. you left your other job completely to dedicate yourself to your idea, you will need to be a little ruthless and harsh on yourself. You will need to recognize that maybe despite your best efforts things have simply not worked out the way you hoped. Sure, give it another few weeks, few months, but do put limits, "In six months if I don't have at least X customers, I will stop this and try something else." Maybe you don't know what else to try at that time and maybe you have to go back and get a job meanwhile, it doesn't matter. As I said before, you will have learned something, that's for sure!

A possible complication here is if you have a partner or maybe even more than one. If things don't go as planned, each person will undoubtedly have differing ideas about what to do, how long to persist. This can lead to huge problems as just imagine that you walk away, but your partner persists and in two months things are going great guns. However, this partner now says its all theirs, it was their hard work and persistence; you left so now you have no right to anything. This is where friendships are tested, when there is money involved.

So once again these things, although they are far from your mind when starting out, must be thought about and best written down and agreed upon before starting your business. Mark my words, you will regret a laid back approach later. It's the same as someone giving you twenty bills of ten pounds each one. Out of politeness you don't count them, you trust the person and you feel rude counting it in front of them. Don't feel rude! It is the most polite thing to do in order to avoid the problem of a miscount on their part and then a much larger problem later. Always count any money in front of them; always inspect any goods that arrive before signing for them.

We all get lax and trust people, but then we all feel stupid and embarrassed or maybe even angry to go back to them when there is an error, but the error is ours for not doing things right in the first place. It took me forty or more years to learn this, but anyone that thinks you are rude for counting or inspecting is not going to be as successful as you are.

As far as success and recognizing it, it is said that when Mr. Micheal Dell of Dell computers made his first million, he pretty much said to his staff,

"Well done, now lets get on and make the next one."

As for Richard Branson of Virgin fame, now there is a company name for you, I've heard him say that every penny from his first million went back into his business in order to grow it more and more.

So each person has a different idea of what success is and each person measures it in different ways and at different times. Sometimes you are simply too focused on things in order to worry about whether you are successful or not. I don't at the same time think personally that you need to reinvest every penny in order to become even more successful, but yes you certainly need to invest if you want to keep ahead of the curve.

The companies who had and have the philosophy of "If it isn't broke, don't fix it." may still continue to make money and maybe grow and grow, but as we have mentioned, a lot of this is down to pure luck. If no one comes into your market with new ideas, then you are lucky and you can continue without evolving or developing, although I would not recommend it as a viable approach in business or life.

It only takes one person or one company to see you have not kept up with or better yet, gone ahead of the times, in order to see an opportunity and that's all they need to potentially enter your market and maybe take it away from you. The history books and FT articles are no doubt littered with examples of this happening.

To give just a few examples here: Blackberry, Nokia and the whole British car and once upon a time the enormous British motorbike industry. Blackberry had a big hold over the business sector hand held device / mobile phone market. In certain markets they were leading in sales of devices in the none business market also, this is before apple entered for the second time. Yes apple did have, way before the iPhone, another attempt at the personal organizer digital device and it failed terribly, the apple newton if you want to look it up, although it was back in the 90's.

In the UK, younger people craved for Blackberries due to their messaging program, BBM, as we have mentioned. These customers did not use or even know much about Blackberry's superior email ability, something their business customers no doubt raved about; I certainly did. In the US and South America it was also a huge hit and had a decent percentage of the entire mobile market at that time, late 90's early 00's.

Blackberry should have in fact been a threat to Nokia's dominance at that time, but they simply did not develop their products fast enough or diversely enough to really attack Nokia and maybe they did not even try to, maybe they were happy in their particular area, albeit a slightly none descript cross over area as it was. The Canadian company was doing very well and were perhaps happy enough to be as successful as they were at that point, and I'd say they rested on their laurels somewhat.

They certainly did not foresee Apple coming in and practically wiping them out, although it took a while, certainly in the business market where Apple did not have a product as secure or functional as Blackberry's for email at least, or messaging for that matter. Maybe Blackberry thought they were developing at a sufficiently fast rate and perhaps they felt Apple would not be such a threat, especially with their units being so expensive, as they were!

However, someone, or more likely a whole board of someone's really didn't do their jobs very well at Blackberry. In fact, ever since that moment that the iPhone was released we could say the same of Blackberry, they never managed to catch up or respond correctly. However, the last four or five years at Blackberry has probably been pretty impossible, they are so far behind now in terms of market share, is it possible for them to ever recover the position they had. Can even Nokia do it, it certainly doesn't look that way!

The head of these companies has a job probably that was just as impossible as being Liverpool Football Club's manager ever since about 1991. After a period of renowned success, it is always very difficult to continue and even improve upon it. What makes this even more difficult are the expectations of those who witnessed and enjoyed the success, i.e. the stockholders and users in the case of Blackberry and Nokia, or supporters for Liverpool.

It is difficult and some would say impossible to stay on top of the tree forever, but with the right people and investment in those people and in your products and development, there is actually no reason why you can't stay on top. Although again, I could say this does require luck, or at least the lack of bad luck.

Lets move on and talk about how to keep ahead of the game, which is basically the same plan as how to develop and grow your business. We don't need to worry too much yet about huge competitors eating our market share and if any of us manage to get to the point of having such success as any the successful or even failing companies mentioned here, well we wont have done too badly for ourselves will we?

7. Business Development / Growing

Assuming your business has brought you some income, if income is your goal, or maybe a growing customer base, if that was your goal, then how now do you further grow it?

Expectations

You need to have made them in order to know if you are now ahead or behind your expectations. If our friend Henry had expected to sell twenty burgers, fries and onion rings a day, but after two months of opening his business he was just selling on average fourteen a day, well having set this expectation should give him the impetus to work harder to get at least to his goal.

No doubt his original goal would have had much to do with the costs he had calculated. Naturally, his original costs and other numbers may have changed and hence, this may mean that even selling twenty burgers etc. Now means he is not where he hoped he would be. Either way, his focus hopefully remains as he set his targets and his business is not where he knows he it needs to be.

On the other hand, if his original numbers were just on the back of an envelope and very slap dash, he may be quite happy now with fourteen burgers and what have you a day; he may now even lay back a little. This is not a real entrepreneur though, a real entrepreneur will set targets and keep going until they meet them and then, they will no doubt simply raise them higher.

In my own mobile phone business, our targets were forced upon us. If you remember, we were contracted into accepting 300 phone lines, whether we liked it or not and hence, our perhaps unrealistic target was to fill each one of those phone lines with new students entering their masters programs between August and October, where we really concentrated on just three business schools with a total potential market of about 400 or so. In this case, we needed to get 75% of our total target market at the first attempt, this is similar to launching a breakfast cereal in the UK and hoping to get about forty million people eating it. Well it's not quite the same, but you see it was always going to be a stretch.

So yes 300 customers in three months, that was one of our targets, but the other and possibly more important target was the overall spend of the customers using these 300 lines. It was no good to us if we managed to get customers for each line, but then they only spent five euros each. You may recall the minimum spend with our provider was fifteen euros each line, i.e. a total spend across all the lines of 4,500 euros / month. However, this did not mean 4,500 euros of profit for us, as clearly out of these 5 euros each person spent, we had our cost prices for each phone call made and each text message sent.

For example, lets say a customer from their 5 euros per month spend uses half of this on "cross network" calls to Vodafone and the half on "on net" text messages to other Amena users. Well we had a quite high cost price for the cross network calls and a relatively low price on text messages that remained on the Amena network. On the 2.5euros worth of Vodafone calls, maybe we made a profit of 0.75 euros and on the 2.5 euros of Amena texts, maybe we made a profit of 1.25 euros. Hence, from the 5 euros spend, our profit could have been a total of 2 euros.

Quickly completing this example and assuming all 300 customers did the same, we would have had a theoretical profit of 300 x 2 = 600 euros. However, the total spend would have been just 300 x 5 euros = 1500 euros which would have been 4500 – 1500 = 3000 euors less than the minimum so in fact there would have been no profit as Amena would have charged is the minimum 4500 euros a month.

I hope that makes sense, its quite simple really. Until we reached or passed the minimum spend, we would in fact make no profit at all. Once we reach the minimum spend and fulfill our condition with Amena, then the profit counts lets say. In the example used of 300 customers spending just 5 euros a month, we actually would have lost 3000 euros a month!

At this time, we can forget about mobile data usage as it was not a big thing at that precise moment; the providers were perhaps aiming for it to be the next big thing, but it would take another couple of years before they got their wish. Which brings to mind the phrase, "be careful what you wish for." As when they did get their wish, it wasn't long before clever companies like Skype and later whatsapp, introduced technology which allows you to make phone calls using data instead of the normal voice service of your provider, hence, making it much cheaper to make these calls and reducing the profit margins for the providers.

Getting back to the point, I'm not proud to say we didn't reach our forced upon us goal in the first three months, i.e. we did not get 300 customers, instead we got about 180. Maybe we should have been more worried, but we were not as during each billing cycle we could already see how much these customers were spending. At that time the average spend of a customer in Spain on their cell phone was about 20 euros each month. However, we were already seeing the average spend of our customers was over twice that amount at about 40 euros a month and hence our provider was quite happy with us overall, even though not all the 300 lines had traffic on them.

In terms of our own internal profit we had been slightly inventive. Knowing very well our customer base and what their habits would be, we knew that most of their phone calls would be to other students from the same group, basically to other customers of ours. As with any mobile network in any country, the calls places between their own customers, or "on net" as they are called, are always cheaper than those that require you to enter the network of other providers.

Quite simply providers charge each other to use their services, so when you make a phone call from one mobile network, like Vodafone, to another one, say Orange, Orange will charge Vodafone for connecting that call on their network. Where as if a person with Vodafone calls another person with Vodafone, this cross network charge doesn't exist.

We had the ability to create our own mobile phone plans and decide the pricing for each type of call and message. Hence we could charge more for calls to other networks and less for calls to our own customers, and this is what we did. In this way we encouraged our users to bring us other customers, as it would be cheaper for them to call each other.

In fact, talking about expectations, it was my own expectation that once we managed to get a customer from a certain school, this customer would help us get other customers. Remember, all of our customers were foreigners arriving to a new country and with no friends or family there. These students were very dependent on advice from others who had already arrived. Besides which, they also wanted to make friends and what better way to make a friend than to help them and give them advice.

In fact, this particular expectation was more than exceeded when many of our first few customers came back to the shop and personally brought us several other new customers! They had maybe met up for a drink and had recommended our service to their new friends and as their courses had not even started yet, they had the time to accompany their new friends to our offices.

This is all part of customer service and not so much our expectations, but we are a company that always tried to go way above and beyond simply providing a mobile phone contract. We offered advice on areas to live in, internet providers, cheap flights around Europe and well, our office became almost an information center. We had been through what they were going through now and so there was empathy and we could share our experiences with our customers and they were all too happy to receive them.

In all my previous employments I had always tried to become friendly with my customers. This for me is part of human nature, but for you if it isn't part of your natural character and you can't think of it as a good way to behave in general, then you can perhaps think about it in terms of your business and its success.

If you have a poor or none existent relationship with your customers, then they will find it very easy to complain about your service, if the need arises. They will also find it very easy to change your service for those of another company, if a slightly better offer comes along. However, if you have struck up a good relationship with them, the chances are any small error or problem is not mentioned and it would also really take something quite major to get them to leave your service and seek or accept another.

I would go so far as to say that for my part, the most important aspect of our business and all my businesses that followed, was customer service. Yes you want to have competitive pricing, the latest technology or whatever, but you have very little if you don't have good customer service and a good relationship with your customers. Many cheap airlines have great prices, but have terrible customer service. Yes, people use their services for the pricing, but if another company comes along with similar pricing and better customers service, they would loose their customer base in a moment.

I should add here that our business was, if you remember, in Barcelona, Spain. I had witnessed at first hand the idea of customer service in Spain and more so in Barcelona, which for me, and for each customer I ever had there, was the worst we had ever experienced. People treat you as if you are doing them a favor by eating at their restaurants, drinking at their bars, or using their cell phone or any other service.

Even in banks, its as if they are paying you to leave your money there in your account, when in reality they give you no interest at all on most of your accounts in Spain. It really was quite incredible and to this day it's still bad, but little by little they receive training from foreign companies and it is getting better.

So although in one way our business did not reach it's expectations in its first period of three months, which was the major intake of students, in another and maybe more important way, it did actually reach and surpassed its other goal. The only issue was that we had another 120 lines without use or customer, but these lines came in handy when the following January came and many exchange students from other schools and countries arrived. I would say from the 120, we probably used about 90 or 100, so everything worked out quite well.

One thing we did in our pricing plans was to have a minimum spend of X euros on calls to other users of ours. These calls were almost free to us, so as we did charge for them, we knew having a minimum use for each customer guaranteed us a certain amount of revenue and profit each month.

Naturally in Henry's burger bar he could not really have an obligatory minimum spend for each customer in the way that we did. The best he can do is assume that each person that enters will at least buy one hamburger, as it is unlikely they would just come in for a lemonade or a portion of fries on their own. Henry's business is a lot harder to predict than mine was, at least after the first few months. A mobile phone company signs you up and commit you to a contract for 12, 18 or even 24 months. They also, as we did, commit you to a minimum spend each month. Hence I knew where I was financially with my business after the first few months; I knew how the rest of the entire year or even longer, would go.

For Henry it's harder to predict his customer's patterns, at least until he gets a full year under his belt. Then and only then can he really know what effect holiday periods have or perhaps cold snaps, rainy evenings, valentines day etc.

Developing Your Business

Now you know whether you have reached your goals and expectations, you can look at what to do next. What should the end result of developing your business be? Well it depends a little on the type of business you have, but you can perhaps develop your product, or develop and increase your customer base. Either way you would hope to increase your revenue or potential revenue, otherwise, why bother developing at all?

Well, even if you don't grow anything, but still develop, it is still a valid exercise as we have already seen. If you don't do anything, you don't develop your product, make your customers happier, you may be risking loosing those customers altogether. As we said, standing still is not a good option, even if the money keeps coming in and your profits stay the same, or even increase. You never know what's coming, or who is out there setting up something to eat away at those profits.

In Henry's case, what can he really do with his product? In fact, until he gets his restaurant relatively full during the week and more so at the weekends, you could argue he doesn't really need to develop so much his product, but his sales. Assuming his current customers like his product, then perhaps he still needs to get word out there before he looks at changing his recipes or improving customer service.

In the sexist world we still live in, maybe a few pretty girls in Henry's Burger T-shirts, giving our flyers outside of his location will help drive more customers his way. He could also do a 2 for 1 offer, or a free dessert, or any other marketing ploy he can come up with. What he needs are bums on seats and hopefully once he gets a bum on a seat and they try his tasty and slightly different burgers, these customers will want to come back.

He can also hope that his burgers and his customer service are so good, that each bum on a seat will recommend his burgers to other people and that's more customers for him without having to do anything additional. If this is not happening, he can think of a way to encourage people who eat at his restaurant to tell others about it. Perhaps he can incentivize them by offering a free meal for them if they bring someone else, or both parties get a free drink for example. The possibilities are almost endless of what Henry can do in order to increase his bums on seats, he just needs to think about them and try them to see which one works best.

In order to see which of theses methods works best, Henry should start recording and analyzing his results. Only that way will he see which methods to continue with and which ones to terminate. Keeping track of customer's sales information is very important in any business, as they say "information is power" or was it knowledge, but in this case its the same thing.

Now maybe when there is bad weather, such as rainy evenings or when there are snow covered streets, Henry's place looks like a graveyard on a Friday at midnight. Clearly he can't control the weather, not even Bill Gates can do that, and so what can Henry do to drum up business? Well Henry needs to think of solutions to all his problems, this is part of what business development is and being in business in general we could say. To combat the weather perhaps Henry should look at offering deliveries to his customers so that they don't have to get wet on the way to get their burger and he may open his doors to a new group of customers that don't like eating out that much anyway.

Today there are of course various companies set up that dedicate themselves to the process of ordering and delivering your food, so perhaps Henry would also use them and add himself to their list of options. While we are at it, he could also look at providing food for small events and meetings. Finally, he could advertise the option of throwing children's birthday parties or indeed any kind of parties at his establishment. This is not a new idea, but MacDonald's have not managed to copyright it either.

Finally he could also team up with maybe a microbrewery or other providers who may be keen to gain access to his location and customers and offer their products there and hence, share some marketing and location costs. With all this and with Henry's own ideas on top, we would hope that Henry would develop his business and increase his revenues.

Moving on to my own business, or rather our business, we also needed to develop our business and in particular our product. We were two young, well kind of young minds at 29, and we should have been able to come up with new ideas that other mobile companies were not doing at the time, especially for our niche market of international students.

Well I certainly did have what I thought was a novel idea. Back at this time Skype was possibly just in its infancy if it existed at all. Maybe some businesses were using it, but it was certainly not well known or even dare I say it, reliable at that time. In fact the whole idea of Voice Over IP was something not many people knew about and less understood, myself included.

What I did have personal experience of were these international calling cards, how else was I going to call home while living in Spain and indeed in the USA before that. Mobile operators at that time were charging somewhere in the region of 1.5 euros a minute to call internationally from Spain to the USA for example. Hence a half hour call would cost 45 euros, and hence just in order to catch up on events at home you would be paying almost one weeks rent at your shared accommodation.

Here was an opportunity for us to help our customers and also make some money. Firstly we naturally started to sell the calling cards, which allowed our customers to call internationally from their cell phones at far reduced rates, up to 90% cheaper than calling without the calling cards. My partner even wanted us to start sending the calling card information via text message as soon as a customer needed one. That was good customer service, but it was a bit antiquated. Also what if the customers needed a card at 11pm on a Saturday night, well I got on well with my customers, but working at those hours would be pushing my relationship with them.

What we needed was real a development here, an innovation; we needed to do something no other company was doing. I just had to think of a way to combine our mobile service with the calling cards service and make it as seamless as possible. At that moment the customer had to call a number, then enter a pin code and then enter the international number they wanted to reach. It was a bit of a mess, even if it did save them a fortune.

So just like before I started this business, when I just had the idea in my head, I did my research and racked my brain over and over. During my research I learned about phone calls been sent over data lines, the same lines that send the internet around the world. Upon searching the same internet I came across several companies that provided this service. By coincidence, one of these companies was run by some English guys down in the south of Spain, close to Malaga. Hence it was quite easy to talk to them and see if they could help me.

This company actually made their own calling cards and offered the option for me to have my very own calling cards to sell to my customers and to people who weren't currently customers at all. Here I would have a new source of revenue and as the calling cards would have all my company info on them, it was also good and free marketing.

However, useful as this was, and even though it made me a little more money, it did not solve my problem of wanting to make the whole process easier to make international calls at a much reduced rate. I kept on researching as I was now sure it could be done and eventually I found another English company based in Spain that could help me.

This company would normally not deal with someone as small as myself, but I convinced them I had potential to grow and I also offered to improve upon their current cell phone service pricing, by offering them my own service. They agreed and we very soon had a system where by our customers could save their international numbers in the phone's memory and call them at the touch of a call button; there were no longer any need to enter pins to then enter the number; there were no calling cards involved.

Without a notion of being biased, I can say with all sincerity that what I was offering was by far the best customer service of any mobile phone company, and with the most competitive overall prices in the country. What other mobile company in Spain spoke English to its customers at that time and responded by phone or email to their customers requests and facilitated them to call most countries in the world for 10 cents/min to a land line. What other company gave advice on living arrangements and knew what their customers were going through in their busy MBA programs, well again, none at all is the answer.

Other providers in Spain were basically robbing their international customers blind with their international call charges and even their prices for international text messages were twice the price they were from other countries in Europe at 60 cents each one. We charged around half that price and would have gone lower, but our provider also charged us a rate that was almost as extortionate as what they charged the general public.

So I had successfully managed to develop our product quite extensively and for that I was quite proud of myself, but you can never really stop doing this if you want to keep ahead and hopefully keep growing. The better your product the more appeal it will have and to more people, and hence the less likely they will look else where and the more likely new customers will look to you, as long as they know about it of course, but then you are back to marketing.

There were other problems with our product though. For you to know the problems with your product or service you simply need to listen to your customers. If you can't hear them, then you need to ask them. This you can do with a small survey, but you must be careful.

I can imagine Henry will put, as many people do, a suggestions box on his premises that perhaps you only notice on the way out, and at that point very few people are going to stop at the exit, look for a member of staff, get some paper and a pen and spend a few minutes filling out their suggestions. It is perhaps better than nothing, but I'd say only just, and I would add that the only things that end up in suggestion boxes are relatively severe complaints, not general recommendations.

These days' restaurants will now perhaps bring a small questionnaire with customer's bills that asks their guests to rate their service and their food, and then there is a comments section for recommendations. This is certainly better than the suggestions box on the wall at the exit, but I still think in your business you can do something better. You just need to think a little more.

Firstly think to yourself, how many times have you filled out that little piece of paper? Once, twice or ever in fact? How many times have your friends or family done so? Again, I'd say you don't get a real and representative feedback from this way of doing things.

You may now think that as your business or Henry's is so small to start with, perhaps he as the owner should be around the customers, introducing himself and asking how was the food and the service? But again, if you think about it, having just met the owner of a restaurant at your table and you are with friends or business contacts, and he asks you how was everything, will you really complain about something? Unless your food had a major floor, would you simply not just say as most people do, that it was very nice?

Unless you are the exception to the rule, I think you will find very few people will be honest or even bothered to give any advice or suggestions and least of all to the owner, when confronted with him for a moment at their table, while they are eating. No, you must be cleverer than this if you are really interested in people's opinions and want to improve.

I will give you two suggestions, one is very cheap and one is very expensive, but you really should come up with your own. The first option is to really train your staff, your waiting staff in this case, to recognize and inquire into any issues. If they are genuine and friendly and interested when they ask at each stage of the meal, I believe they will get a much better feedback. However, if they are disinterested when they ask the questions or worse still, don't even give you the feedback of the customers, then this will clearly not work. It's up to you higher the right people, train them and show them how important the customers are and that you need this feedback in order to stay in business.

Now the next option is just a random one that popped into my head, although as with most things, if you search online, I am sure some locations and even restaurants are already doing this. You need to make it maybe not fun, but at least interesting for the customers to give their feedback. You could have a cheap "ipad" on the table that flashes or makes a sound, or asks them directly at each stage of the food how it was. Then all they perhaps have to do is answer back or press a button and leave any comments they wish. It's far more likely to work than a piece of paper left in with the bill at the end.

Naturally when you get the results, you need to analyze them carefully and maybe look at any outliers with caution, but as this is your first business, I imagine you will be there present most of the time and hence you should be immediately involved in anything bad that shows up. If even a relatively small percentage is saying your burgers are a bit salty, or your tomatoes lack taste, well then you know something needs to be done.

As I had quite a good relationship with my customers, its possible many of them did not tell me of any issues they experienced, but by the same token, some of them actually would tell me. The main two issues our customers had were firstly with the delay in receiving their monthly bill from us; it was arriving half a month after the end of the billing cycle in some cases. This was partly down to our provider that gave us the bill about seven or eight days after the month end, and then partly down to our own billing system which took another several days to produce the bills.

Our billing system was made by my partner and ironically, although wanting to spend money on flyers and a website, he had not suggested spending money on someone doing us a billing system that could produce the customers bills at the click of a button and email them straight out. I was in a difficult position though and could hardly pick a fight with my partner, so I did let this drag on when really I shouldn't have done.

We were now making money and had our customers for the next 12 and 18 month periods and these customers would give their opinions to other new students the following year, hence by not saying anything, I was harming our business growth potential and development. Still in the end this situation resolved itself, as you will see later.

The second real problem the customers had was with our coverage, or really our provider's coverage as of course we were just rebranding and selling their service. To be quite honest, I myself had never experienced an issue with the coverage, but this does not mean that I should ignore my customer's opinions; I should and did investigate the issue.

The issue in fact was that the students in one of the schools we provided service to, ESADE where I studied in fact, had some classes on two underground levels. Naturally in order to get a signal underground it is something quite difficult in any location and maybe unfair to expect a company to have it. It's almost like expecting to get a signal in a lift, it just doesn't happen. You will always have some customers with unrealistic expectations.

However, the problem here was that another provider, Vodafone in this case, they did have a decent signal underground at this building. In fact at another building where we also had many customers, IESE, which was very close by, they had a large device that basically increased the signal and it seemed to work for both buildings.

So you can imagine in a group of 150 students what happens when someone received a phone call and all the others look at their phone and see they have no signal. To be honest, the largest Spanish provider, Movistar, did not have signal at these locations either, but this did not help us much; we had to do something.

Quite simply I contacted our provider and explained the situation. They eventually sent an engineer to the location and tested the signal on the various levels and recommended a repeater be installed. In order to do this I of course needed to contact the school and get permission for this work to be carried out at their premises and well, the whole process took about 4 months or so. At the end of it and after a few tweaks, our coverage at ESADE's building was as good as anyone's and on any level of the building.

At the other building, IESE, things were a lot more difficult and as the building had a contract with Vodafone for them to keep their apparatus on site, and then their staff had a contract with Movistar, they were not so interested in helping their students and even less so in helping our business, so there was little we could do in that case, but we tried nonetheless.

As our business was in amongst such a close nit community, which as we have seen is a good and a bad thing, this issue in the other building of IESE was bad for us. On their internal forums the students could and would comment that our service was friendly and easy, but coverage in lecture theatres 2 and 3 was none existent, for example. Now some students would say this doesn't matter as if you are in the middle of a lecture, to receive a call is not so important and actually not allowed of course. Where as other students will complain about everything.

In fact at IESE business school I remember a conversation with a lady that was the student liaison officer, a nice American lady who had worked there for maybe five or six years. We were talking about a few complaints, maybe one of them was the coverage underground at that school, or the fact the 0900 numbers were expensive, something we did not control. She made the following comment;

"Don't worry too much, here I can tell you that at least once a term I get some student come to me in order to complain about the temperature of the Coca Cola in the drinks machine; its too cold or its not cold enough." she said.

So while customer feedback is important and must be taken seriously and investigated, you also have to have some common sense and perspective. If you are producing a Ford fiesta and your customer complains about not having electric cup holders, well, you could remind them, although maybe should not, that this is a fiesta and not a Bentley, and it is priced accordingly, but you can see my point.

Once you are happy with your product, although as I said, you should never be fully happy and just as with a Porsche 911, you should strive to keep on making small improvements, even if most people don't even see them. Perhaps now you are more financially stable, you can explore the idea of spending a little more on marketing techniques, which may be as simple as an advertising campaign, although as we have seen previously, this is something that needs to be examined before launching into it.

Another thing you can do is diversify, although for what we are looking at in this book, i.e. new start up businesses, I can't imagine that you would be looking too much at diversifying your business so soon. When you are an established business then this may be more of an option to develop further.

Having said that, sometimes opportunities arise, in fact if you are really putting yourself about with your business, with your providers, your customers and whoever else, then conversations occur and opportunities sometimes do present themselves. You should obviously have an open mind, while at the same time dedicating yourself to your business.

Back to my mobile phone business where I was not looking to diversify or do anything out of the ordinary to expand; things were going well and it was growing of its own accord as our reputation grew, so too did our client base. Nonetheless, when I was looking for a Voice Over IP (Voip) provider for our international calls and had found these Spanish based English guys and their companies down in the south of Spain, I did see a chance to diversify a little.

One of these companies was providing cheap international calls to some of the large ex pat community down on the south coast of Spain. These people were using his service to call back home to the UK, Germany, Sweden or wherever from their fixed lines. They just needed a slightly special phone and they could save a fortune on what Telefonica was charging for these calls.

As I was now going to be offering these same cheap international calls from a mobile phone it occurred to me that this guy had a customer base of a few hundred foreigners who, while they were not my current niche target market, they presented a new and different niche target market. However, rather than diversify myself so early and maybe look at open up a competing office down there on the south coast, I decided to work with this person I had just befriended.

I offered to provide our mobile services to his company so that he could then sell them on to his current customer base. Naturally I would give him better pricing than I gave to my direct customers, as he would have to resell and make some money. He was very interested and the idea had not occurred to him before, but now it made perfect sense for both of us. It would be some extra income and limited risk as we would be using each other's services and would be crossing over invoices from each other.

This did indeed work very well and the relationship lasted for maybe six or seven years. But like all good things they generally come to an end and perhaps we will look at that later. However, it just goes to show that getting our there and putting yourself about, talking about your idea or in this case your business, can lead to other opportunities, maybe even very related like this one was. All you have to do is recognize these opportunities. Or well, all you have to do first of all is get off your backside and get out there!

8. Reacting To Change

Sometimes change can come early in a businesses life, and maybe even before your idea has even been developed into a business. Here we will take a little look at the types of change that can crop up in a business. We can look at some general changes that we have all seen and I will also be giving examples of real ones that have happened to me.

External Changes

In the mobile phone industry, especially in Europe, there are always changes. In fact, in any technology related sector by definition there should be constant developments and hence there will be changes practically all the time. Sometimes a non-tech sector may also be effected by tech and have to react to change. For example, watchmakers today who are not of the level of Omega and Rolex may well feel under attack by the market shift of tech companies going into watches.

Apple and Samsung now have their watch offerings as well as several other much more competitively priced options from Chinese based companies. Naturally and for most of us, having one watch to wear during the day is sufficient. So for those who already have a Tag Heuer or even a Citizen or Swatch watch, but are also now attracted to buy an electronic intelligent apple watch, well this means they will no longer need their analogue watch; you cant wear two watches at once can you? Yes okay you can, but I hope you wouldn't.

So how do these traditional watch makers react to this change and market threat from Apple, Samsung and the likes? Admittedly not everyone is interested in a smart watch, but there will be a percentage that is interested. The most obvious option for these companies is to offer their own version of these watches, but clearly that's not so easy. An analogue watch company does not have Apple's expertise in technology and cannot compete with such a monster of tech.

Not to worry though, in China and probably beyond, there will exist many smaller tech companies who can make similar products to apples and are happy for you to brand them with your own marque. So Swatch for example would just need to work on some great designs and also work in conjunction with a tech company in order to produce "their own" smart watch.

Going back to the mobile phone business, but still talking about apple's influence, this company has managed to force external changes in many industries. Not just to the markets of laptops, desktops, MP3 players and now watches, but in my case they also brought about quite some changes in the mobile phone world. The first real iPhone (that was not the apple newton) was indeed a hit, but it took another few models before it became practically a must possession for even those who had to spend a whole month's income on one.

What did this mean for the mobile phone industry? Well, the days when an operator could afford to give away a handset with the contraction of a new line for 18 or 24 months were coming to an end, at least in terms of these higher end phones. The previous values we spoke about were on average 130 to maybe 150 euros. For that price you got a very good phone with everything you could hope for.

However, Nokia were the first to perhaps introduce us to the idea of spending quite a bit more money on a phone, offering us such amazing features as 2 Meg pixel cameras and then better music capabilities and higher memories. Then, just a few years later it seemed as if people suddenly got fed up of pressing buttons and so touch screens were a must. In order to get an apple touch screen iPhone, you would have to lay out about 500 euros, which was a big leap from even the better Nokias at that time.

Obviously the service providers could not afford to give this kind of money away, not unless customers were signing up to spend in the region of 60 or 70 euros a month and more for close to two years. I was not too worried about the larger companies though, I was worried about my own company. Up until now I had managed to pretty much negotiate free or almost free phones for each new line I added. Even the recycled lines I now had, the ones that had already been used to 18 months, I was able to get a decent discount when I needed a new handset in order to reuse that line, when a previous customer had left us and left Spain.

Hence, a good part of my profit came from the selling of these phones, either to my customers or to resellers down the dark alleys of Barcelona. I looked at this side of the business as my yearly bonus; it was never taken for granted, but always very welcome.

Eventually iPhones changed the mobile phone industry for everyone. Other companies tried to react and create their own touch screen devices. My beloved blackberry tried with the money and persistence of Verizon / Vodafone to come up with a competing touch screen product and they did, the blackberry storm, about a year or two later than apple. However, their product was big and bulky and not as user friendly. I bought one on ebay in the US before it arrived to Spain and it actually never worked properly.

Apple got themselves into such a strong position with consumers that they could now demand a percentage of the operating profits from the mobile network providers, from those lines using their phones that is. This would never have been dreamt of a few years earlier and I know business is business, but well, I don't like people or companies that take too much advantage. In some places where I have lived and even some good friends I have had in those places, there are always those that try to take advantage and it always leaves a nasty taste.

So how did my company react to the iPhone, a product I had saw first hand in the US before it ever arrived to Spain. Well it was becoming clear that this was going to be huge, but I myself had been using a blackberry for around a year or so at this stage, and with me wanting to answer my new customer's emails with as little delay as possible, almost at any hour of the day or night, the blackberry was the best option around, including the iPhone. This was about three years after I had started the original business.

I guess I had the choice to either embrace the iPhone or have a food poisoning type bad reaction to it and keep as far away from it as possible. To be honest, although I respected the first iPhone I saw, it wasn't for me personally. I really liked my blackberry keyboard and being able to type fast and comfortably was an important mobile phone characteristic for me, as it was for many, many people back then. To this day I still can't type as fast and reliably on an iPhone as I could on a Blackberry.

Despite my personal opinion, the iPhone was starting to arrive to Spain and Europe, but it was still not as big as Blackberry was and it was certainly more expensive. Hence, the decision was pretty much made up for me; there was no way I was gong to try to convince customers to spend so much money on a handset. I decided to side with Blackberry and for those few Americans arriving to Spain with their iPhones, I would have to be brave and try to convince them of the local benefits of using a Blackberry instead.

A few things were running around in my mind as the next wave of entering students were only a month away from arriving to Spain's airports. One thing I had realized from studying our customer's call data was that the average length of a call was literally around 30 seconds. I imagined the general conversation would be something along the lines of,

"Hey, how are you? We are meeting tonight at the black pig pub on Manery street at 8pm."

"Ahh ok great. I will be there. What an interesting day today in class; I learnt so many important things."

"Yes, me too, I'm so glad I paid seventy five thousand dollars to do this course, its wonderful."

That informative conversation would have taken about the 30 seconds I was seeing and the other thing in Spain at this time was that there was something called a connection charge, in fact I believe there still is once you step out of included minutes. On top of this, the service providers charged you the whole of the first minute, whether you used it or not. We were charged both of these items, so in turn we also charged our customers for them.

Off at a tangent now, but you will see why in a minute. I had lived and worked in the US for a couple of years in my twenties and as I was quite bored most of the time, or maybe the fact was that I was boring most of the time, I did spend a good bit of time in my apartment. It's never that easy to make new friends in a new country and it does require a lot of effort. Anyway, the point is that I got exposed to AOL, America On Line, which was all the rage back then. Remember the film "You've Got Mail" with the excellent Tom Hanks and the adorable Meg Ryan?

So, apart from an email service, AOL also had a huge customer base for the instant messaging application, which in those days was only available on computers. I hesitate to say it, but maybe it was even before Microsoft's messenger program and anyway, it was probably about the biggest application of its sort at that time. While bored in my apartment, thinking about the girl I was in love with, Jessica was her name, I spent a good bit of time chatting or rather messaging on this AOL program. Those were the days, thinking about Jessica, dreaming about Jessica, text messaging with Jessica, but alas, it was not to be. In this case, bad timing or bad luck was something I had too much of.

Anyway, messaging via these type of programs was something I was very used to doing, as was text messaging. However, each text message cost money back then whereas using these chat applications did not cost money, at least once you bought a monthly data plan, something the service providers wanted you to do.

So looking at peoples monthly invoices and seeing how much they were spending on these short calls and text messages, I realized that it would be much better for them to use a chat application; it would work out cheaper in the end and they could write to each other limitlessly. Each short call was costing them for argument's sake about 0.3 euros. And let say they made about 3 a day, so that's 90 a month, which is equal to 27 euros.

A months data plan at that time was costing around 15 euros, saving them almost half and giving them limitless messages. The other advantage was that they could use their instant messaging to contact other people in other countries and hence the expensive international texts could be reduced. They could now keep in touch constantly with friends and family back home without spending a fortune.

Back in about 2005 or so I would say Google was the email of choice for most international MBA students. Yes some Americans still had yahoo or hotmail, but the large majority had Gmail and I knew this as in order to be a customer of ours, you had to register on our website with your email as your username, something I saw on my blackberry every time a new customer registered.

In your Gmail account, Google very cleverly had added a chat feature for all of their customers and it was right there beside their inbox, in fact it was almost impossible to hide. You could see when any of your contacts were on line and you could instantly chat to each other, without having to bother sending an email.

Fortunately for me Google now had their eyes on the mobile market and their chat feature was available on various platforms, including blackberry. At the same time, the mobile service providers in Spain were realizing people were starting to make fewer calls and so they were now quite keen to sell blackberry handsets, along with the compulsory data plan of course. In fact, I think for each data plan my company contracted we got a free blackberry handset worth about 175 euros. So now all I had to do was to convince our new intake of students of the benefits of using a blackberry and using instant chat applications that could be Google's or Blackberry's own BBM.

At that time all new customers generally met with me at sign up and as I had been in their situation before and maybe due to a hopefully trustworthy personality, most of them followed my advice. All I had to do was to explain that they would be avoiding high call and connection charges and would be able to chat with those back home, if they either had a blackberry or simply opened a Gmail account.

The other advantage you now know of also came into play. Once I convinced one or two of the first few customers to take a blackberry unit, then they themselves helped to convince the others as now it was also in their own interest. The more of the students that had blackberries the better it was for them as the more they could talk with, or rather message with each other instead of having to call.

I was not and would like to think I never did, convincing anyone to do something that was not in their best interest and financially and socially speaking it really was in their best interests. Besides, Blackberry was quite big back then in the US and also in India and South America, at that time it was still far bigger than the iPhone. If we took these three regions alone, they probably made up about 50% of our customer base and so they fully understood the benefits. In fact some of them brought their own blackberries with them in order to use them in Spain.

Skipping a few steps, but getting to the point, my company managed to get about 70% of its users to use or buy a blackberry phone that first year we introduced them, and of the remaining

30%, probably a further 90% did take a blackberry after originally deciding against it. Only one person from memory every felt "tricked" into taking a blackberry and I gave her the money back she had spent on the purchase.

To show what a success this had been, one customer sent me a photo taken with her blackberry at a fellow classmates BBQ party one Saturday afternoon. They wrote to me on BBM, "you did this". The photo they had sent showed about twenty students all stood around the BBQ and all quite close to each other and yet not one of them was talking to another, instead they were ALL there stood chatting away on their blackberries. Quite sad really, but quite an achievement and very good for business! Clearly the customers were happy with their purchases; addicted to them I would say, just as I was.

External Regulatory Changes

When I talk about business owners not wanting to accept that there is an element of luck, well here maybe I can explain why they really should accept it, while looking at things from a different perspective. If Apple had just released the iPhone after investing hundreds of millions of dollars on it and with a full order book and a skyrocketing share price, can you think of something that would potentially ruin them?

Well, I certainly can. If several recent US government studies suddenly illustrated that a particular technology used in the iPhone or maybe in any mobile phone, but that was lets say more prominent in the iPhone, was harmful to our health, this would be the worst news Apple could hear. This news, especially if it then led to government action being taken on public health grounds would end Apple's mobile phone business and maybe have further repercussions for them.

Of course we are only giving an example and yes, maybe Apple could go back to the drawing board and alter their technology, but sometimes when a name is damaged, there is no coming back from that. When someone is accused of sexual harassment, even if they are later found to be innocent, I would acknowledge that in my own mind I'd still think they had done something wrong, which is unfair of me. This is the world we live in today, where social media virtually tells us what to think, very sad, but almost true.

So here all I would say is that there are many things out of our control where we can be lucky or unlucky. As we have seen Apple did venture into the hand held device many years ago, around about the time Palm was quite big, as was Psion and even Nokia gave it a go with their personal organizer, the Nokia 9000 communicator, one of which I have on top of my wardrobe somewhere. Apple's device was however, a failure compared to the others and that's why you probably never heard of it, the Newton. So, not even apple get it right all the time.

In this case I believe they could not get their hand writing recognition software to work reliably and by the time they perhaps did get it more reliable, the reputation of the device was tarnished and Steve Jobs canned the unit after about the 6th year of its life and it had been developed for a good few years before that also.

In fact, just on that subject, Apple were later convinced with their iPhone that people only wanted a phone that someone could hold and manipulate, i.e. type on, all with one hand and in their later years they refused to make a larger screen unit, like the Samsung Notebook. However, again they got that slightly wrong as many people did want a larger unit and Samsung were selling millions of them, so eventually apple admitted defeat and produced their "plus" versions.

We all like to think we know what's best for our customers, but we can only ever have an idea and we must be open minded about it. I for one would say Apple are not the most open-minded company out there, they are far too closed for my mind and don't relate to their customer base well. For me personally, and I do like their products, they are still a company that tries to tell you, or more likely force you what to do and what to use to do it. However, this shows I don't know too much as they are still the largest company, based on stock market value, in the world. I feel pretty sure this will change over the next 5 – 10 years, if they don't change, but again, what do I know?

Back to what I thought I did know, the mobile phone business. Yes, here there are many regulations and governing bodies all over the world. There also used to be very many differing standards around the world, but these days we are more aligned. Not withstanding this, Europe is always a difficult place to do business, with local standards and rules and then the risk that the EU bodies that sit over everything can change things for all countries under their umbrella.

In Europe, or the united states of Europe if we can think of it that way, the mobile providers in each country have their own way of charging their customers. In some countries the providers charge a connection fee for each call, as Spain does. This charge is on top of the price per minute and is almost hidden and not considered by the users. In other countries they perhaps charge a minimum duration of 30 seconds or a minute, something again that Spain did actually, but later they introduced per second billing.

However, one thing all companies within Europe did was charge their customers quite outrageous charges for using their service when outside their home country, but still within Europe. This still happens but now just when you travel further afield in the world. That as it may be, the European Union was not happy with the charges been made by these mobile operators and they received thousands of complaints from users who would find themselves with huge bills when they got back from their two week holidays abroad.

Naturally the European Union could only look at charges levied within Europe, although in reality there is no reason why it costs more to roam, i.e. use your phone outside your home country, in the USA or Australia than it does within Europe. We think of these other countries as being further away and so it's more reasonable that they charge us more, but that's rubbish. The price to use an Australian mobile phone network is the same as it is to use an Irish mobile phone network if you think about it. They have the same antennas and the same billing methods and can give the information just as quickly and cheaply as anyone else.

In any case, the EU likes to be in control and in some cases, rightly so, and they were not going to let these European mobile providers overcharge us Europeans any longer. Hence, after many meetings and many proposals and many days, weeks and months, they came up with a plan to reduce these rates. They forced all the providers within Europe to all charge the same rates and those rates would get lower and lower over a certain time frame, in reality during various years.

They also introduced a maximum spend while roaming in Europe of 50 euros, if you activated the service. The providers had to warn you when you reached that limit and give you the option to have it as a maximum cut off limit, but this was only for data. You could still spend much more than that on calls. While roaming you are of course charged for incoming calls as well as outgoing calls, something many people are not used to as it does not happen so much, mainly only in the US.

And so slowly but surely the roaming call and data charges the mobile phone operators had been making a fortune with were reduced. Eventually, we got the point in Europe where it now costs the same to use your phone in another European country as it does to use it at home. In fact, in terms of international text messages, it is actually cheaper now to send them from outside your home country than it is from home.

This was a pretty big regulatory change and the providers fought hard against it of course. They did not want to see things from their customer's point of view, instead they only saw things from their profits point of view, which is shame, but that is how most business work of course, especially large businesses.

For my company, and just as it should be, we had no choice in the matter but to follow suit and charge what we were being told to charge. However, our provider was quite unfair to its customers, including ourselves and they tried for some time to use the letter of the new laws instead of the intention of the new laws.

For example, the EU had said data should cost 1 euro per Megabyte, however, they did not say any more than that. Hence, our provider very unfairly set up their tariffs in 2 Megabyte blocks, so that the minimum charge would be 2 euros, even if you only used 0.1 Megabytes of data. I'm sure many people naturally complained and eventually the EU or their own conscience or fear made the providers adhere to the law and charge per Megabyte.

This regulatory change was no doubt a loss in very profitable revenue for the providers, but just imagine if my business was set up, as was the original idea, to provide a mobile service for international travellers. I would have been making money from these high roaming charges, by offering a service, phone or sim card, that charged a lot less than the main providers did.

If this was my business, and as I said, it could easily have been my business, then in this case, with the new regulations, my business would have been in ruins and it has to be said, through little fault of my own. Yes, there will be those that say it's your own fault for not keeping up with the times and developing your business with the times. This is true, but even still, there are some occasions when external factors like these come too fast to possibly react and you are at risk of loosing everything. It's not always so easy to develop and keep up and less so keep ahead, but yes you have to try.

This is why I say there is always luck involved and I was lucky I did not go down my original mobile phone renting idea. Not withstanding this, I could see with these new regulations that things were changing. I could clearly see people were using more and more data and making less and less phone calls and so my whole business model and pricing plans had to change if I was to still make money.

When you are basically a reseller, your whole business depends on that of your provider and their pricing to you. If they are making less money, they will no doubt raise their prices to you and unless you do the same to your customers, you will make less money. Still, lets leave that defining moment for a little later.

You may think external changes along the same lines as these could hardly affect old Henry or even myself, once I was later in the hotel business. Well, I put to you the phrase "as mad as a cow". In the UK and other countries of course, when mad cow disease was at its height, I am sure there were very few people eating hamburgers, even if the restaurant reacted quickly and made it clear they were only now using imported beef. They could also start to focus on chicken burgers, veggie burgers and introduce temporarily other dishes, but undoubtedly Henry would be affected quite seriously and through no fault of his own.

As for my hotel, there could have been many external factors, some regulatory and some not, which would have had a large affect on the business. My hotel was in a slightly unstable country and a country where terrorist groups still hit the headlines quite often. Most of our guests were foreigners and so if one of the said terrorist groups happened to plant a bomb relatively close or even just in the same city, which has happened, then my trade could drop of quite significantly.

As a hotel offering its services mostly to foreigners, the initial and maybe only option would be to change direction and try to accommodate more locals. The locals are more used to such events as bomb scares and in any case they still have to travel for business. Also a slight price modification may get the hotel back on an even keel, although many other hotels would no doubt also reduce their prices.

In terms of regulatory changes, the government and varying bodies could certainly affect our profits quite substantially. As I recall there was not one but two taxes we had to pay to be able to have TV's in the bedrooms. These taxes were very high and most of our customers didn't even watch the television, as they did not understand the language. Nonetheless we had to pay rights to artists on the television and in addition rights to music that was played in the programs, even though the cable provider would have already paid these in the first place.

The government can also affect us directly and not just through third parties. In Colombia where my hotel was based, you would charge sales tax to a national of that country at 16%, however, for a foreigner, they were exempt from this tax. This makes quite a difference to the attractiveness of your pricing, especially for longer stays. Some hotels incorrectly did charge this 16% to foreigners anyway, and just hope that the guests in question did not know about this law, and many of them didn't.

All in all, you have to be prepared and in some cases you can actually be ready for some external changes by following the news around your industry. As soon as the first case of mad cow disease hit the UK, that was the time for any burger bar there to start preparations for using meat from other countries and maybe widening their product line. Yes it would be unfortunate for the UK beef industry, but business is business.

Once the European Union first started looking at roaming charges within the community that was the time for mobile providers to look at various scenarios and start to strategize. If you sit back and don't keep in tune with your industry, you may find yourself left behind.

On that note, the English company based in Malaga that I had made contact with was owned by someone who formerly owned a large and successful print company based in London. He had about eighty people working for him and had every kind of car you can imagine. However, he then left the business more and more in the hands of his managers and before he knew it, his company was slipping and sliding down a slope, which his non-stick shoes could not get him back up.

He lost the company and lost his wife and lost all of his cars, not to mention property. When I met him, this successful businessman was living in a 2 bedroom rented apartment in the south of Spain without a real asset to his name; he had effectively lost everything. Still, he was actually happy enough, which is just, as if not more important than all the rest! So you need to keep your eye on the ball, or have someone you trust with your very life in charge of your business, and such a person is very hard to find.

Finally back to my phone business and Apple. Another problem arose when apple simply could not supply their phones in time. Apple would generally press release their latest phones in September, but maybe not have them available, even in the US until mid October and then to other markets like Spain until mid November. This was an issue as my new customers would mostly arrive in August and September and they would want their new iPhone at that time.

Fortunately no other Spanish provider could give them one either so they either took an alternative, or in the name of good customer service and reaction to changes, we also offered to lend them a used blackberry and the the Sim card and then when Apple got the latest iPhones to Spain, they could simply pop down and collect their new phone when we got them. This was a small adaption on our part, which we were far more able to do than the larger companies. Flexibility is and should be a large advantage of smaller companies over larger ones.

9. Breaking Up Is Hard To Do

If you did start out with a partner or even a small group of you started the company together, you should know from the outset that it isn't easy. You should at least be aware of the statistics, even though you don't want to be one of them. Yes, you should still go for it, if you don't, you wont even get to be a statistic and that would be worse!

Why Do So Many Partnerships Fail?

Depending on where you look for the statistics, you will find anywhere between 50 and 80% of all partnerships fail within a few years. However, to balance that out, there will also be a large percentage of single owner companies that also fail. The simple difference here is that if you are on your own you maybe have something more to prove and you also don't have anyone telling you when exactly he or she thinks you have failed.

When there are two or more of you there are naturally two or more opinions on when is the time to throw in the towel. If you think the time is now, the chances are you will convince the others to give it in. If however, one of the others thought the time was actually before now, the chances there are that he or she will already have convinced you to give up the ghost. That's one simple explanation for why some partnerships fail before sole ownership companies do.

There are many, many more detailed reasons why this could also be the case and perhaps these are worth considering before you go into a partnership. I am no expert in partnerships, although I have now had three of them in my business ventures. All of them have failed to a certain degree, but at least in two of the three cases we managed to remain friends, which has its place also.

My opinion is that a business partnership is in some ways like a marriage and in fact, during day light hours you will potentially be with your business partner far more than you will be with your husband, wife or life partner. I would argue that you don't really want to spend this much time with someone if you don't get on with him or her pretty well, and that goes equally for business or personal relationships of course. You don't need to be best of friends necessarily, but you need to find them reasonable and you need to be able to communicate well with them, just as you do in any relationship.

If early on in the idea process you can see sides to their character that are already rubbing you up the wrong way, you can multiply this factor by two or three by the time you spend several hours a day with them, and pretty soon you wont want to be with them at all. Based on this, the same as in marriage, you could say that it's best not to rush into it until you get to know the person very well. Yes you could get lucky and the "love at first sight" ideal may turn out to be true for you, but it may also not turn out to be true and that may lead to a nasty divorce.

Hence, try to go into business with someone that you like to be around, or at the very least can easily support being around. I would not worry too much about the "opposites attract" saying because I don't actually think its true. I've yet to meet a married couple where they are really opposites of each other, this just sounds like an awful lot of hard work to me. At the same time, you don't want a mirror image of yourself in business, but you do need to think about things in a relatively similar fashion. You may reach differing conclusions, but the thought process should be quite similar I feel.

Having said that, if you are a marketing specialist and you form a business with another marketing type, then unless the business is a marketing agency, you will need the skills of others. I disagree with those that say you should not be with someone with the same skill set as yourself. However, you certainly need to recognize what skill sets you are missing from the partnership and where you will find them. Will you invite someone else to join or will you outsource these other needed skills.

Also in this case of two marketers, you don't want to be duplicating your efforts so you need to divide the work up and be open to accepting some responsibilities that you may rather not do. If you both want to cherry pick and decide the companies advertising, but neither of you wants to cold call potential clients for example, then there will very soon be a problem. Flexibility is important and all involved must bend over, maybe not backwards, but at least sideways.

Another problem can be effort put in by each partner. If you are young free and single, you probably have more time and maybe even more energy than a married partner with children, who perhaps keep them up the odd night or three. It's very hard to allow for this in partnerships as you may feel that you are putting in all the effort, but the other partner may feel that although you dedicate more time, maybe they feel they work more efficiently than you do and so they actually achieve the same results as you do.

This brings us back to where we spoke about a document of reasonable expectations to be signed by each partner before you enter into the partnership. It's difficult to put in exactly the same effort all of the time, but you would hope things generally balance themselves out, if not, grievances may arise.

Certainly in the case where one partner is really not pulling their weight and is hardly contributing any discernable effort at all, the other partner(s) will probably reach for the dissolution agreement if they can't make said partner change his ways.

I remember going to a friends wedding in Puerto Rico when the referee, or the vicar in this case, was giving their informal speech on happy marriages. Quite ironic from one that is not allowed to marry and has no personal experience of the concept, but still, I guess anything is possible.

In her friendly speech she said any relationship was like an empty box. The box was just waiting for each person to contribute and put something inside it. A good relationship would be one where the box remained pretty full most of the time. However, if only one person was putting things, in this case effort, into the box, and the other person was perhaps simply taking things out of the box without putting back much at all, then the box would become quite empty, quite quickly.

An almost empty box would be a bad relationship. I think I've had a box so lightly full that it could virtually blow away in the wind, but lets not get too personal about my personal life. Naturally there will be times when one partner needs to take out of the box and is suffering in their lives and needs the box to be filled by their partner. At this time the other partner must be understanding and generous. However, where in business there is generally no love in the relationship, hence this understanding will have its limits and is not to be abused.

The simple point is that all the partners must try and put a similar effort in. Allowing for their ups and downs, the box should always be at least half full and hopefully that will keep the relationship afloat!

So the business could actually be doing fine, but if one or more partners feel they are being let down by a fellow partner, then they may seek to dissolve the partnership. When a business is making money this can make for an interesting experience. If the business is going nowhere but down, then it helps quite a lot as more than likely no one really cares if it continues or not. As I said, they say, you only really know your partner when you divorce from them!

Other reasons partnerships can fail are when roles are not fairly or happily split. There maybe an ideas type person who likes to start things, as I myself do, but then this person could really dislike the day-to-day management and organization of the business. Perhaps he now wants to be off and start something else, or simply isn't someone to sit down and do the nitty gritty.

Well this can work out if the fellow partner is happy to get on with this far more unfashionable part. However, there are few people who are happy to let the other have all the limelight, not while they do the shoveling let's say. There must be seen to be some flexibility on both sides and perhaps some overlap of the roles chosen. If you are not happy with the role you have been chosen for, it's best to say so sooner than later.

Related to this reason is maybe when one partner feels bigger than the rest of the band, maybe the lead singer now feels they do not need the base player and drummer; any other base player and drummer will do. We have all seen this down the popular music years and it happens in business too. I would say it was pretty much what happened during apples first few years or so, when Mr. Jobs left his fellow partners and went it alone.

Who is to say he was wrong, he did go on to be one of the richest and most successful men ever to live, although I still maintain its still quite a lot to do with luck. However, even with all his success, it's widely rumored that perhaps he was not the happiest of the original partners. Success and money are what you are probably looking for, why else would you start your business in the first place right? Well, sometimes this can go to your head and you change as a person without even realizing.

Ronald Wayne, one of apples three founding members sold his 10% apple stake for about 800$ and also all his rights for 1500$. He claims he was happy and I am sure he probably had a less stressful life than Steve Jobs, but he must slightly regret selling his share, which today would be worth around 75 Billion US$. I'd say Steve Wozniak is perhaps the happier of the three original partners and well, although not as wealthy as Mr. Jobs, he did okay for himself and later continued doing what he enjoyed and with a smile on his face.

I think the very fact that Steve Jobs reportedly lied to Wozniak while working at Atari and basically stole money that Wozniak had earned, this says a lot about their relationship. If one partner is the sort of person who tries to take advantage of the other, well that's never really going to work out in any relationship. You need mutual respect and honesty.

The simplest reason for a partnership not to work is that the business was just not working, the idea wasn't developed enough or the competition was stronger than expected or, maybe a recession hit at the wrong time, not that there is ever a right time. Besides this, as we have mentioned, different partners will no doubt have different expectations and without repeating myself too much, this will inevitably lead to problems.

The Failure Of My Partnership

You may have noticed in the last few chapters I had consistently referred to the mobile phone company as "my company" rather than ours, well that's due to the fact that during the events we have discussed, our original partnership was dissolved and I then started my own company. This relatively short period of my life was one of the worst I can remember; I don't think I've ever been under so much stress, not outside of personal relationships at least.

So here goes, here is the story of how I hope your partnership does not turn out, but how mine did turn out. This is naturally from my side and no doubt there is another side, but the facts remain the facts and they on their own are probably enough to illustrate the situation. However, I may mix my own opinions in there also.

Although I previously mentioned the signs were there, ie.e when my partner wanted to give away a % of our shares in the company to his wife for having done a few hours work, the real problems started around four months after we got our first customers. This was only about seven months or so after we had formed the company and did all that running around for a location and negotiating with the provider.

To put it all into perspective, at this time I really felt that I had done almost everything, although I never said that at the time. I had the idea, I had developed and developed the idea. I had made contact with Amena, our eventual provider. I had made the pricing plans, the marketing info and the website. I had made contact with the schools and done a good job of it. Apart from moral support, when he was in the country, the only thing my partner had done was to set up the billing system, which as we know was slow in the extreme. Okay as the Americans say, that's my beef, over and done with.

I think my partner would have preferred to be working on his own idea, but for whatever reason he wasn't and so maybe thats why he had not shown as much effort, as it was all my work. I don't know, but as I said, I was happy to have someone to share the risk, share the nervousness, although yes it would have been nice to have someone to really take on half of the workload.

It was Christmas time and I stayed in Barelona rather than going home. I myself had not been home for about 9 months at that time, where as my partner had probably been back to the UK with his wife four or five times. I was not out partying either, I really was working and thinking all hours I could.

After Christmas dinner we started talking and the problem came from a simple discussion over our pricing plans, which I felt were a bit unfair to our customers. I thought they would eventually lead us into problems with said customers and this is not good when you are trying to grow a business and rely on your customers to bring you more customers, which is what had happened so far.

At this stage money was being made and we were drawing a salary of about 1500 euros / month each, which is not too bad after only 4 months of running the business and we could easily have drawn more, but we were cautious.

In our pricing plan, we were forcing our customers to have a minimum call usage between them; these calls cost us nothing. In general our customers surpass this minimum usage, but some customers had more friends apart from other customers and hence did not always use the minimum spend here.

I wanted to reduce or even eliminate this tactic, which was basically guaranteeing us a good profit. I had analyzed the data and I felt we were making good profit without this and it made very little difference to the overall situation. Hence, for the risk of annoying a few customers, who may then go on to create a problem for us, I said we should modify this tactic.

My partner was initially against the idea and wanted us to carry it on for a while longer, but then he waned and we agreed to modify the price plans, or at least that's what I recall. I hence made the modification on the website and felt that was a done deal. However, when the very next customer came to the office in January, my partner stuck with the old plan and I politely reminded him we had altered it. There were no fireworks, even when the customer left, my partner said nothing, so I thought nothing of it, apart from the fact that I thought my partner was always on the side of profit rather than providing a fair and good service, which I think allowed us to make profit in the first place.

At the same time I myself had managed to get us an appointment with Vodafone, who had better coverage and maybe better handsets than our current provider. This was quite an exciting development and it could help us springboard our business onto another level the following year. Again, he had not helped at all on the development side, it was maybe as my Spanish was better or more likely that it was not his idea that he really was not interested in moving forward with the business, or so it seemed.

However, before even going to that meeting, my partner had a surprise for me! He came in one morning and said he wanted to talk to me. He said he had been to a lawyer and an accountant and had a document for me that he wanted me to read. This was a complete surprise to me, totally out of the blue, but I read it.

This document started with a long list of problems he had seen in the business. The list started with what terrible communication we had between us. It also stated how undermined he felt when I had corrected him in front of a customer regarding the plan changes. It also talked and complained about the unprofessional website and flyers and some furniture in the office which I had procured. And then at the end of the document came the big shock, there was a proposal for him to buy the business from me!

He had been to see a local accountant and had calculated a value based on a certain methodology. He said if I wanted to add anything to it or make any changes to the assumptions he had made, to just go ahead and do it.

The first thing I said was,

"Can we talk about this?"

To which he said "no". I followed that up by the obvious,

"So you are complaining about a lack of communication, but we are here every day together and you have never communicated any of this until now and when I want to talk about it you say we cant. That seems a little ironic don't you think?"

He had made his mind up; he wanted out, or rather he wanted me out! This brought my next slightly angrier reaction.

"So you want to buy the company, the company that really started from my idea and from all the contacts I have made us at all the business schools in the city. You want me to move to Madrid and leave you my company here in Barelona."

I forgot to mention he said I could go and open an office in Madrid, but not part of the current company. This was as I had mentioned several times as Madrid would be a good location to expand into, although we were not really ready for expanding at that time; we had only just got off the ground.

Well I was not happy as you can imagine, this was what I considered to be my baby and I felt the only thing he had really contributed was the billing system, everything else was down to me. In any case, at the weekend I studied his numbers used for the valuation. The methodology for calculating the value was heavily influenced by the cash flow and the potential number of students at each school. Most of his numbers for students at virtually all the schools were incorrect, so that upped the value a little in my favor.

However, the main thing he had completely forgotten about were the 120 cell phones we had in our huge safe. So I put down a nominal and fair value for selling these phones in the Barcelona back streets, something I could easily do and this really altered the valuation.

If memory serves, his offer to me was about 15,000 Euros, plus returning my original deposit at the bank, held by our provider. You may say 15,000 for a company having just started was a good return, but don't forget I had worked night and day for several months on this business. In any case, when I added the value of the phones corrected the student numbers, his own method now put the value of the company to be about 120,000 euros. I presented him this document and that's when the real fun began.

He came back to the office the next day and said,

"I have thought about it and I accept your offer of 120,000 euros for my half of the company. Until you come up with the money I suggest we work alternate days; today is your day so I am off. I will be here tomorrow and you can come in the following day."

Naturally I explained I was not making him an offer, I was simply putting his own calculations up to date with the real numbers, which he could verify if he wanted to. It was pointless, he was not going to negotiate and off he went. Now we arrived at about two weeks of an impasse, he was determined to split the partnership and he wanted the company. In fact he even went so far as to tell Amena, the provider I myself had found and created the relationship with, that he was buying the company and that I would be gone! He was so sure of himself and clearly sure the business would be even more of a success.

This was turning into a soap opera and not a lighthearted one either, and now it was about to take a turn for the even worse. My well brought up, privately educated business partner and someone who I thought was a friend came into work on one of my days, when he was not meant to be there at all and he accounced,

"I've decided I'm going away for a month or two. My wife's parents have a house in the South of Spain we are going to spend sometime there. Good luck with running the business, lets see how you get on without me." were his words to the best of my memory and once again, off he went!

This guy was at the time about 35 years old, five years older than me and I just thought, how childish. Then as if that was not shocking enough, and it was, but what I did not know was that he had also been to the bank where we were both co-signers and he had taken the bank book, which meant the bank would not let me do anything with the money already in the account. This meant, as he possibly well knew, I could not pay our provider, which was very unprofessional and not befitting an MBA or any other graduate. I was also annoyed with the bank as they offered me no help whatsoever, but there was little I could do without a lawyer.

As my partner well knew, he left me with some quite big problems. The end of the month was upon us and he was the one who had set up the database for processing the customers bills from the raw data. He always did the bills on his own Apple laptop, which he had of course taken with him, so he had really left me in what he considered to be an impossible position.

Ah yes, I almost forgot. My friendly and reasonable partner had also emailed all our customers, every last one of them, and he had told them he had now left the company in an administrative sense and that any problems they should contact me. He presumably wanted to cause a panic amongst them, thinking perhaps that they may loose their phone lines. I honestly to this day cannot believe that all of this even happened.

This was all a bit like a James Bond movie where the evil guy straps Mr. Bond down and a laser is slowly cutting through the table on which he lies. Said evil villain guy walks off, expecting Mr. Bond to die. However, in about 24 books and films Mr. Bond has yet to die, so there was perhaps hope for me?

One way or another I felt absolutely terrible. I could not believe this was happening and I wanted to believe there was a solution to this, but sometimes people are just so unreasonable and negotiate in such an unethical manner that there is little you can do. I in the mean time had told Vodafone what was happening in the company, i.e. I told them the truth so they would not be expecting our company to sign a contract any time soon. This was something else my partner did not appreciate; he had wanted me to lie.

So, here I was; Amena had sent out the bill that consisted of thousands and thousand of semicolon-separated numbers in a huge text file. Somehow from scratch I had to get from this blur of information into a relatively attractive looking bill for each one of our customers and then email it to them. Only this way would they pay these bills and only this way would I have money to pay our Amena and hence, enable the business to continue.

I was no expert at using and even less had ever created a database in my life, and to be honest, I did not feel that now was a good time to start learning. What I had done previously however, was learnt how to use spreadsheets to a decent level, as anyone who had studied chemical engineering would have done. This was the only approach I felt I could take to calculate the bills using some very long and complicated formulas in Excel. Remember our provider billed us using their formulas, but we billed our customers using our own plans, which were totally different.

I worked pretty much straight through the night, as when you get the bit between your teeth with something like this, you don't like to let it go until you finish. After several hours I could certainly see that it could be done, but that it was going to take a pretty long time, too long in reality.

Soon after that I remembered that excel had macros, which is where the program records your actions and then repeats them for you. So fundamentally I just had to produce one bill, while recording the macro, and then use said macro to then produce each one of the other bills, changing the names and email addresses.

In the end, I got all two hundred bills produced in about two days solid. They were saved in PDF format, something we had not used before and something which eliminated complaints from customers that could not see their bills my partner had produced on his apple laptop, which at that point in time still produced word documents which were not 100% compatible with Microsoft based computers.

I felt quite proud of myself in that I had processed and sent out all the bills in less than half the time my partner had previously taken each and every month. The customers even gave good feedback about the new format, which was far easier to understand and I also explained about what was happening in our company, which the customers were sympathetic about.

That month's money came into the bank and the provider was paid on time without a problem. A major catastrophe had been avoided and I saw that I could run the business, every aspect of it, without my partners input at all. I could pretty much run the company working about 1 hour a day and then a few days sold at the month end to do the invoicing.

My partner and I were at this stage not communicating at all; he was outside of Barcelona relaxing with his wife or planning his next move in this unfortunate game, which I did not view as a game at all. I still wanted to work this out, even at this stage and even after what he had done to me.

I imagine he soon found out that the bill was sent and the business was fine without him, so his pan of forcing me into selling up or giving over my share to him was not going to work. As a result of this he consulted again with his lawyer and the next thing I knew I got a letter to the office from his lawyer. I don't recall much of what it said other than that this lawyer would like to speak to "my lawyer" which I did not have of course.

At this time I had only one other commitment, which was teaching GMAT at a local school, something I had started to help me get some income while my business ideas turned into something that produced income. One of my students was a lawyer and he offered to help me, for a fee of course.

Eventually and after another month of high stress and even feeling that a whole year of my life had been wasted, my partner came to some of his senses and dispensed with the lawyers and we sat down together to see if we could work this out. I think he did not want to continue paying his lawyer to do something he could possibly do better himself, i.e. reach an agreement with me.

He now asked me how I proposed to resolve the situation; I gave him two options. One was for me to sign a non-compete agreement for Barcelona such that I would not be able to set up a new business in the city nor approach the very schools I had the contacts at. This offer of selling my half of the company had a value to me of let's say about 65,000 euros, plus my initial capital at the bank, hence 50,000 euros more than he had offered.

The second option I gave was for me to sell my shares to him and I could then do whatever I wanted; I could set up office next door if I liked and additionally I would take with me ten customers of my choosing. This option would only cost him 30,000 euros.

The first offer I made, which would involve me leaving for Madrid was viewed as outrageously expensive and that the business would never be worth that much and hence, we agreed upon the cheaper option meaning we would now be competitors!

This whole process, from his ten reasons for wanting to split up the partnership to the signing of my shares over to him took about four months and so we were now into May. During the months of March and April I had already set up my own new company. I had met once again with Vodafone and had negotiated a deal with them, while also keeping the previous provider.

Now "the game" was on. I had kept the previous provider so my partner would not know I was negotiating with the new one and I also had a slightly new product offering, which I wont go into details here about. There was little time to find a new location and so I decided to initially work out of my apartment, which was very well located. I had a large sitting room that looked quite professional and it was well separated from the bedrooms, so this became my new sales office. My flat mates worked all day, so no one generally came into the apartment during working hours, although those working hours were going to be very long.

All my contacts in the schools soon knew what was going on and so they knew that this year there would be two mobile phone offers for their students, plus the normal big three companies of course. If this experience had taught me one thing it was to delegate and know your areas of expertise and at the same time know your limits.

I had previously managed to do the website, the flyers and in the end the billing system all on my own, but this time would be different. Now I knew the business had good potential I was happy to pay someone to do these things, but I was also happy to spend a bit of time to get the right people who were also in a similar position to myself, i.e. foreigners in Barcelona who were professionals but were looking for some scraps of work to keep them going.

I interviewed various people and eventually found a programmer with huge experience, who had given up his job at Orange in the UK to move to a more relaxed life in Spain. There was also a designer from Scotland who was looking to make ends meat while he tried to piece his life together with his new Spanish girlfriend, whom he had left the UK for.

Together we made an almost identical copy of Vodafone's UK website and a billing system that meant I only had to hit a button to get the bills generated and another button to email them out to the customers. The flyers that were designed were of a cartoon style design, which I really liked and did not look at all cheesy, something the far more expensive ones from my partner had an air of. I thought everything looked great.

Going Too Far

So the battle lines were drawn, the soap opera was soon too reach its Christmas episode with no doubt an over the top and dramatic climax. At this time I had put my website up live to do some testing, even thought it was not finished. The license needed for what we were doing, i.e. reselling telecoms services, had been applied for. This was something we only realized we needed when dissolving our partnership. So I was ready for business, slightly nervous, but ready. I also knew I had the best offer now I was with Vodafone.

So as the new intake arrived to Barcelona I had the best offer out of the two. I had the best service provider and the best prices since I had got rid of the unfair part of our previous billing practice, which had in part caused this whole mess. I had been busy though and was behind my partner in terms of contacting the schools; here he was well ahead of me at one of the schools, the largest one, IESE. However, luck favors the brave and the just, doesn't it? Probably not, but it was about to favor me in any case.

On the day that this school, IESE, had their induction day, I went up there with a guy I had hired to help me for this year, initially part time only. Vodafone had given me some free red carrier bags with their logos on them and I had managed to squeeze our of them some free gifts, quite expensive looking key rings, which sound cheesy, but they were pretty cool actually. I also put in a free map of the city, free coffee and some other bits to bulk the bag up a little.

We walked into the school, with no prior warning but this time we asked the person in charge of the induction if we could hand out these carrier bags. The lady I spoke to surprised me when she said,

"Ah, you must be Peter, nice to meet you. Well why don't you make a presentation in the assembly hall at the end and then you can hand the bags out as the students leave."

This lady clearly had email contact with my ex partner and had arranged that he would hand out his flyers this day also. She mistakenly thought I was my ex partner! (Peter is not the real name of my partner by the way.)

"Ah no, I'm not Peter, I'm Gary, Peter's old partner. The company has changed a little, but we offer the same service ..."

And without going in to too many details she was happy enough to continue to allow me to make a presentation. I got very nervous about making an ad-hoc presentation in 25 minutes to about 250 people. I found myself as quiet as a corner as I could and I tried to think of a few funny lines to say during my 2 minute presentation. I was not a fan of public speaking and to this day I am not a fan of public speaking.

However, when I stood there, red faced and almost with my voice almost shaking in front of the students my nerves soon disappeared. In the next 2 3 4 and 5 minutes I had made all of them laugh quite a few times, even the staff that were stood there watching managed a few laughs. I drew to a close and my new employee was at the door to give out the bags and flyers to all the students as they left. In the end we had about 5 bags spare and we gave them to the lady who had helped us.

Now we left IESE and went to my home office awaited our first customers of the year. We had no way of knowing if any of these students would come down to us or not. It was likely that a fair few of them had already bought the easy option of prepay phones and although I had highlighted the more costly nature of these, we still had no idea what would happen, all we could do was wait and hope.

Back at IESE, "Peter" had now turned up after lunch as agreed with by the lady at the school and when she met him, she quickly hid my Vodafone bags behind her back and explained most of the students had now left for the day. That must have been quite an awkward moment, but I wont say not deserved in some ways.

Well, by the end of the week I had about 100 students signed up from IESE, some of which congratulated me on my brief presentation, saying how funny it was and that it had just the desired affect. By the end of the following week, I'd say we then had about 150 of the potential students and a few more came after that time too, so we ended up with about 90% of the potential total available. You have to remember some of the intake were Spanish who had their own contracts from many years and they were never really our target market.

At my own school, ESADE, things would be a bit more difficult as of course my ex partners current crop of students would possibly recommend his service. However, from the total of around 100 none Spanish students, I would say I managed to get about 70. Hence, from a starting point of almost zero compared to my ex companies starting point of around 170 customers, we had caught up with and overtaken my old company in terms of customers. There were other schools where I also picked up customers that did not really like Peter's approach.

I should and did feel quite pleased with myself again. I had certainly got lucky with timings at IESE and a simple piece of luck was possibly the one thing that got me on the way to finally achieving a customer base in excess of 2500! I would say in terms of the international MBA student market at private schools, my company supplied about 85-90% of the market at one point and that is something to be proud of.

10. Knowing When To Move On

Depending on your initial ambitions and how they may have changed over the life of the idea and business, you may be happy now your business is working and you never want to move on. In fact, you may now want to keep and to grow the business and eventually hand it over to your children. Even some of the larger business owners do this, Robert Maxwell and the Glaziers have involved their sons quite heavily in their business ventures. However, everyone is different and some of us prefer to look for a new challenge, while others may even prefer to retire early.

Why Move On?

You may get the chance to sell your business; someone may come along and want to buy it even though you were not even thinking of selling it. This is precisely what happened to me, although under very unfortunate circumstances, which I hope never present themselves to you.

From the outset your idea may have been to set up a business which would be worth a good deal of money with the very idea of selling it, after perhaps not having made that much money along the way. We have looked at this already, but unless you get to quite a large scale, it's not an easy thing to do.

One of my friends set up a business along these lines with the intention of being bought out after a few years. In the mean time their business was making money, but only a very minimal amount, enough to pay maybe what was twice the local minimum wage. It too was a partnership, but along the way they had looked for investors and had got them, so the percentage of the company the original partners owned between them was soon perhaps just under half.

They had a good customer base and business model, but they were just not making as much profit as they would ideally have liked. In fact when my friend decided to move on and go back to look for a corporate job again, I can remember his comment at the time:

"I am fed up of living in my underpants." he said.

Which I always imagined him to mean that he was fed up of living on the bread line. He and his partner were waiting and waiting, looking and looking for some larger company to buy them out, but as I said, its not that easy, you can be lucky or unlucky. The company is actually still running to this day, but with only one of the original partners involved. The company is still not sold but makes enough money for that partner to have a comfortable life.

He will buy the shares of my friend over a certain amount of time and still keep the dream alive. While I am sure that my friend will wish him well, he will also not probably want to hear in a few years time that his old company sold for millions of dollars either, as he would have by then sold his shares for a fraction of that amount.

So in this case my friend moved on in order to improve the quality of his life. He had been living away from his home country for several years and while that can be fun, it can also loose its appeal, especially if you are, as he said, "living in your underpants". And the appeal can be lost even sooner if you were used to living in much better condition before any down scaling of comfort in order to invest in your business idea.

Everyone has their limits and everyone has to make their own decisions, but if you have the option to sell up, then you should consider it. After all, there may be other ideas in you that are just waiting to get out and be explored. Or, as is the case for my friend, returning to a regular commercial job is not the end of the world. There is a lot to be said for a regular salary coming into the bank at the end of the month and perhaps free health care and child and car benefits, plus a pension fund!

In my own case, after I took my partners offer to buy my company out, at what I think was quite a low price, we fought for the next few years as competitors in the same niche market. I know I am not the first person to have this experience and in fact, even in families such things have happened.

I remember listening with amazement to the story of Adolf and Rudolf Dassler, two brothers who founded a shoe company in the laundry room of their family house. Their shoes became very popular thanks to them being used by some athletes at the Olympics before the Second World War. However, a misunderstanding and a lack of communication believe or not, lead to the company splitting up and the two brothers formed their own companies, Adidas and Puma.

The two brothers never spoke to each other again, but the two companies became two of the largest sporting goods companies in existence, quite remarkable. So although I was quite stressed and upset about all that had happened to me, far worse things have happened to far better people. Having said that, I did not quite finish the story, so let me do that now.

After the split of our company and after my initial and self satisfying success, I then had time to look for an office and so I moved my location out of my own rented apartment after the first seasonal entrance of students had occurred. I painted the office myself over Christmas in my new color scheme, chosen by my Scottish graphic designer. The colors were a quite vibrant pink, a more sobering grey, and a classic white. Many people initially frown at the idea of pink in their logos, but it is one of the colors that stands out the most of course, just ask T – Mobile.

I did not exactly relish my ex partner's competition and my idea was never to compete him into the ground or run him out of business. I ran my business the way I saw fit and I made very good money from it. I was the first one out of the two of us to use Voice Over IP for international calls, which I mentioned before, so technologically and cost wise I was a step ahead of him. However, I was sure there was enough market there for our two companies, after all, if one reached outside the private MBA schools, there were around 30,000 foreign students arriving to Barcelona alone each year. However, stepping outside the MBA schools brought more risk with it.

Anyway, I was happy. In fact the good thing about my business was that I only tended to have to work hard for three months in order to reach my sales goals, i.e. get the students through the doors and to sign contracts, but after those three months of arrivals, the rest of the year was pure maintenance and that part was basically admin and almost anyone could do it.

Still, one day, while I was in my comfortable and enjoyable position, but far from being wealthy, the buildings porter passed a large envelope to me. It was from the Commission for the Market of Telecommunications, the CMT, the very body that I had just received my license from in order to be able to do what we were doing, i.e. re-sell mobile phone services.

As I read the first page of this letter, in my intermediate Spanish, I was already pretty shocked. The first page was telling me that this government body had received a claim from another entity that my company was illegally operating in their field. Several claims were made in fact, some of which were as follows:

My company did not have a license / permission to operate.

We did not mention connection charges or VAT (tax) in our pricing.

We were selling below cost prices and hence, they believed this was unfair competition.

There were several other accusations made against my company, and the lawyers who made this case were recommending that the maximum penalty available, which was in the region of millions of euros, be applied to my company.

I was speechless; I could not believe someone would do this to me, but there it was in black and white. Who was it? Well I think you can already imagine whom. Yes, my ex partner was not happy that my new company had got the jump on him and basically outsold and outperformed his company. So after having just got to the far side of a few very bad months now thanks to my ex partner I was about to do the same again.

In the end I got a lawyer to help me and I was very fortunate in that I had just received the license for my new business. Possibly I did not have it when he started this claim with his lawyers, but I had received it by the time the claim was sent to me, and hence it was quite easy to answer that part of their claim.

As regards to the numerous pages he had printed from my website that showed our prices to be missing off that they were plus tax and had to have the connection charge added, well, he had simply taken these pages from my website before it was ever available for my customers i.e. during the testing phase. This was before I had even defined my final pricing, he must have downloaded my site and basically sent it in as it was.

Hence, here it was also easy for me to illustrate that what he had presented was outdated and did not apply, as at that time when he downloaded the site I had no actual customers. It was obviously corrected by the time it was available for potential customers to use. What's more, and quite ironically, I found the brochures his company was using that same year and they did not have the tax mentioned, which was illegal, but again, my intention was not to ruin someone, despite what they had done to me, so I ignored it.

We answered the case against us and although I was quite nervous, the lawyer was extremely confident and he was right to be. The answer came back from the CMT a few nerve racking months later and they agreed with everything we had said. They even noted that if I chose to sell below cost price, which I certainly did not, we could happily do so as we were not a significant factor in the telecommunications industry in Spain, we were after all not Vodafone or Movistar, who had 10,000 times more customers than ourselves.

I continued with my business and on went the battle with my ex partner. The following year though I went to visit Instituto de Empresa in Madrid, IE as it is known, and they seemed very open to the idea of offering my services to their students. I had got the contact there from a contact of mine at another Business school, EADA. As I said, it makes sense to make friends with your providers and contacts if you possibly can.

For the next two or even three years the admissions staff at IE allowed us to send the phones and sim cards down to their office and they would look after them and hand them over to the new customers who were busily ordering them, many of them even before they arrived to Spain. By now I had managed to get my companies name on their facebook pages and in general there was only positive feedback and so most new students followed the advice of the current students, which was good for me.

Eventually I sent someone to open an office in Madrid in an excellent location, directly in front of IE. It wasn't long before that office was producing just as much as the Barcelona office, since there they had two intakes during the year and they also had other masters programs apart from the MBA program.

I was not unhappy to hear that my ex partner finally closed his business, actually leaving his remaining customers completely stranded as they lost their numbers, some of which his customers had been using for five or six years. I know this as several of these customers came to ask for my help, but there was little I could do for them unfortunately. Their lines were the legal property of my ex partners business and he was burning his bridges with Orange.

Actually I met him in the street a few years later and I even bought him lunch, not that he was that destitute of course. He had now started another business, a Voice Over IP business. He had split from his wife and had a few difficulties, none of which I would have wished on anyone. We never mentioned what happened, but although he then lived about five minutes walk from where I eventually lived, I have never saw him again.

When To Move On?

Perhaps not that different to the why to move on, but lets get straight to my mobile phone business again, my own individually owned company. I actually received an offer to buy my company from someone who worked for me during a year or so, after they finished their MBA.

This person came from quite a wealthy family and he could see how profitable my business was at that time. However, the offer that was proposed was that of a similar amount of money that I could make back in 12 or 18 months. At this time I had several staff working for me so I really was not doing that much work myself at all. I was at that point spending about half or more of the year travelling around the world. Nice work if you can get it, I know!

I also knew that my business had a finite life and that one day that life would come to an end, unless that is I did what many true entrepreneurs did, which was invest everything they had made back into the business. I for one was not prepared to do that, I had instead invested in property and although the Spanish property collapse came at just the wrong time for me, I still felt safer having some bricks to my name than a business that had its risks in an industry that was quickly changing, i.e. telecoms. In any case I did not sell, I could not see the point under the circumstances.

Over the period of the next few years there emerged more resellers on a much larger scale. Some of these tried to go after the ex pat market and even marketed in English. One company in particular was started by some ex IE graduates, but with a lot of investment from large Spanish businesses. They did not heavily effect my customer base even at IE to be honest, and I think as a company overall they lost money for quite a while, trying to get a foothold in Spain.

However, by now I had taken a large back seat in my own business and was almost letting others run it, or it ran itself. Very much like my friend and his publishing business. This had the effect that the customer service dropped off a little and now there were the odd complaints, something I really hardly ever had when I was mostly present and on top of things.

Another factor was the iPhone. Eventually it conquered the blackberry, despite my best efforts. Blackberry pretty much self destructed with several delays in software updates and they never got anywhere near the levels that apple were reaching with the iPhone hardware. I of course sold iPhones also and did very well with them, but with roaming charges in the EU now virtually disappearing and Orange fully overhauling the way they priced their services, I could see the writing was on the wall.

I had a meeting with Orange, who were now a far superior company than they were before. Their customer service had improved no end compared to the people at Amena I had to deal with in the earlier years. From my point of view Orange was simply not that competitive any more. Most of the large resellers, some of which Orange were selling their services to, were undercutting them and it was almost impossible for me to compete with these companies and make money at the same time.

I looked at some new plans offered by Orange, but I asked myself, if I was a student coming to Spain, which offer would be the most competitive and attractive? When I was sure that my company was not the answer to that question, I decided it was time to move on.

I kept the company running, even after closing the office for another couple of years, just to keep my staff employed or else they would have had to leave the country as they were South Americans and not Spanish. The business was now not making any money at all, it just made enough to pay their salaries. I was now spending virtually all my time in South America looking for new ventures over there.

I think sometimes a business can be like a casino, certainly if it is in a fast moving industry like mine was. And just as in a casino, after you have won some money, you have to know when to get out, when to leave. I think I got out at exactly the right time, about 12 years after I started. The risks had gone up and the profit had gone down, that's never a good thing. But most of all, when I knew my offer was not competitive anymore, that was really when it was time to get out.

My idea was always to provide my customers with a service that was at least as competitive as anyone else's, but with better customer service. So maybe this is a good time to know when to move on. When things are out of your hands and you simply cant compete or develop anymore to be able to differentiate your product.

Shaping Up

Whether your intentions are to sell up, close up or continue, it is always a good idea to have things working as well as they can. You need people in your business that want to be there and that have a real interest in their job, even if their job is only answering the phone, or opening the door. Almost especially if you are decided to sell, its far easier to sell a business that looks in good shape and is ideally profitable and not too staff heavy.

When I owned my hotel in South America, I had left the running of it in the hands of someone local; someone I felt was capable of doing so. However, for one reason and another the sales dropped off after less than a year and the person in charge really showed no interest whatsoever in rescuing the situation. The sales dropped to about 50% of where they should have been and that basically meant we were now not making any profit at all; we could pay our overheads, but that was about it.

Naturally it was time for a change and in fact I wanted to sell the hotel to invest in another opportunity, but I could now not remove the person running the hotel as they fell pregnant. Rightfully so pregnant employees have a lot of rights. It did not matter too much that this person had not done a good job and had actually stolen from me; they still had their rights of course. That is the way it should be, but sometimes you can be unfortunate.

I had to wait it out and eventually when this person took their leave to have their baby I employed someone to run the hotel that had real industry experience, about 20 years of it. Now all I had to do was sit back, wait and see the occupancy of the hotel to get back to the levels it should be right? Wrong, things did not drastically change, a little improvement could be seen yes and certainly things got more organized, but the hotel was still not making the profit it had done when I bought it, far from it.

Eventually, the replacement person left as the original person came back a few months after having given birth. It did not take long from that moment before I caught her red handed stealing again; quite a lot of money this time. In fact by now I had caught nearly everyone working at the hotel stealing in some way or another, quite sad really. As a result of this the person resigned from their position and a thought occurred to me, why don't I run the hotel?

I had already been trying to sell it without success for almost a year, but with the numbers really not looking too rosy, there was no real serious interest. The last thing I wanted to do, for various reasons, was get involved in running this hotel, but that is what I decided to do. It's what friends told me I should have done several months earlier, but I resisted, as I knew very little about running hotels. Now however, was the time to dive into this new industry.

During the next five months I changed several things, but mainly I changed the pricing structure and worked on the basis that it was better to have the hotel 90% occupied at a low but competitive rate, than to have it 40% occupied at a very profitable rate. Whether the hotel was full or empty, my fixed costs including staff were still the same, and these fixed costs were way higher than my variable costs due to guests in any case. Hence, it made more sense to use this new model.

Every day and night I would be looking at the new bookings and looking at the empty rooms. I felt like Ryanair in that it was better to sell a cheap seat than to have that same seat empty. Before long, our occupation rates went up past 90%, which was excellent for the sector. My presence at the hotel I think helped the staff to maybe put on a better show themselves in front of the customers. Any complaints were dealt with and any comments or questions were now quickly answered.

As I did not draw a salary myself, I had also managed to reduce the wages bill quite substantially by not replacing the previous manager. I also did not steal from my own business, so yes the numbers soon really started to look healthy.

All this coincided with a few more interested people coming to see the hotel with a mind to buying it and now with the numbers genuinely looking healthier, it was naturally a far more attractive proposition. In fact, within a few months I had three people that wanted to buy it; they were almost bidding against each other. However, in the end only one of them turned out to be what I would call a serious business person, even though they made an offer and then at the last minute reduced it, which I would say was not so professional, but in any case, I managed to sell the hotel and it made a profit for its final four months of operation.

Luckily I would say I managed to sell the hotel at just the right time as property prices in the country have been hit there quite hard since the recession that followed started to bite. It's a shame I could not sell my apartment there at the same time, but its rare that you can have everything go in your favor.

11. What Next?

So for whatever reason, your first business is now not in your hands. You closed it, sold it, left it or perhaps it simply left of its own accord, what do you do now? You may say the deciding factor will be why you are no longer in that previous business, but I think the deciding factor is you and what you want from life.

Some People Will Never Stop

If you have watched the film or read the book, Les Miserables, you will recall the character of the prison officer, Javert, who then pursued our hero Jean Valjean. He pursued him until his own death, accepting he simply did not know when to give up. He was such a determined man; the only thing that mattered to Javert was the letter of the law and re-capturing Jean Valjean.

Determination is of course an important quality and I am sure the worlds leading entrepreneurs have it and their staff and family could write books about how dedicated these men and women have been. This determination may well be what made them into who they were and as successful as they are. However, I am also sure that there are many more equally determined entrepreneurs we don't hear about that never really made it; people that perhaps did not know when to quit, like our friend Javert.

What's my point? That's a good question and I would answer it by saying that you need to step back, way back, in order to see what to do next. You should surely take some friendly advice on board, even though many entrepreneurs are really awful at taking any advice, myself included in that group.

Some people cannot accept failure and hence they continue and continue. They maybe fail at their first venture, but are determined to continue with another one to prove to themselves or worse still, to others, that they can do it. This is not a good reason to continue starting businesses. Everyone knows you can do it, everyone that is at least not so arrogant to think that only a few can do it. As I have said many times, ability is only part of the equation; luck is also involved. So of course you can do it, the question is more as to whether it is worth doing or not.

Don't loose sight of what's important. Your own happiness is important, of course it is, but don't think having a successful business is the only thing that can make you happy, that would be a huge mistake. Don't forget the other things in your life, your family, friends, health, security etc.

I recall walking with a friend and businessman along with his family to the cinema. His daughter wanted to go and see a film that was rated at 13 and she was only 11. His mom, the child's grandmother did not feel her granddaughter should be going to see the film at all, so she was making her comments about this to myself. The father was determined to fulfill his daughter's wish and get her into the film and so when overhearing his mom's comments he turned around and said,

"Mary wants to see this film and I'm getting Mary into see this film, are you not part of this team?" he said, in a quite condescending tone to his own mother, which quite shocked me.

His mother then of course said nothing in response; what could she say? I'd not really commented on the matter, other than I imagined they would have someone on the door to check the ages anyway. In the end, we did not get into see the film, although I am sure they soon after watched it at home an any case.

My strange point here was when my friend said, "are you not part of this team?" He is an entrepreneur and like most entrepreneurs I would say the last thing he knows about is being part of a team. In fact, his family is his team, but he is manager and coach and it is he himself who really is not part of the team. The rest of his family are in some way together a team, but he is really on the outside, bossing them around to get what he feels is best for "his team".

Being an entrepreneur, as I have mentioned, does change you, slowly but surely it can make you into something you maybe did not want to become. It's important to stop and take a reality check and see if you are happy with that person. A good reality check needs to come from people who are not afraid to tell you the truth. I recommend do this before deciding what to do next.

There is the other well-known story, a little better than mine, which some say is from Mexico and others from Brazil, but the point is the same in either case. The story goes more or less along these lines:

An American investment banker was on vacations in a small coastal Mexican/Brazilian/Costa Rican village when a small boat could be seen approaching. The man watched the boat come in and eventually the fisherman onboard also came into sight and he docked his little boat. The fisherman had caught several large fish. The American now approached and was amazed by the size of the fish in that had been caught and so he asked how long it took the fisherman to catch them.

The fisherman replied, "only a little while".

The American then asked him why he didn't stay out longer and catch more fish?

The fisherman said he already had enough to feed his family and some left over for his friends too.

The American quite puzzled now asked, "but what do you do with the rest of your time then?"

The fisherman said, "I get up early, I fish a little, I play with my children, I relax with my wife, Jessica, I stroll into the village each evening where I sip wine and I enjoy my time with friends. I am quite busy you see."

The American scoffed and said, "I think I could help you. You should spend more time fishing and with the proceeds, buy a bigger boat. With the proceeds from the increased catch from the bigger boat you could buy several more boats. Then you could eventually have a fleet of your own fishing boats."

The fisherman was the one who now looked puzzled and so asked, "But how long will this all take?"

To which the American replied, "maybe 5 to 10 years."

"But what will I do then?" now asked the fisherman.

The American said, "Well then when you're successful you can sit back and watch your money grow and you could retire."

"Retire to do what?" asked the fisherman.

"What ever you enjoy doing." answered the American. The fisherman stood there, thinking for a while and then said, "But I am already doing what I enjoy. If I retired tomorrow, I would just come back here, with my wife, with my children, go out and catch a few fish, relax, be with my friends and family."

This is the story that makes many an entrepreneur stop and think for a while, but I'd say the vast majority just thinks, "Ah, that's nice." Then they go back to what they were doing; most of them perhaps do see the meaning, which is obvious, but it still does not really sink in.

What Do You Really Want?

Since I closed my cell phone business, feeling it was a good time to leave telecoms, I have had many business people say to me, "Your life is great, you travel all around, you don't have to work, I wish I had your life."

I look at these people, many of whom have their own businesses and are not tied to another company. These people are successful and have wealth and I think to myself,

"You don't really mean what you are saying to me."

In fact recently I have started to answer them back and put them on the spot,

"If you wanted my life you could have it in just a few days time. If you really wanted it you would do it, but you don't want it, not really. If you wanted to you could stop working right now, sell various properties that you have and maybe your business. You would have more than enough to cover your children's education and live comfortably and travel the world and never work again." I say to them.

But you can see just looking at their reactions and their minds working overtime that they get frightened of the idea of loosing their income, loosing their status and sometimes their power. As I said before, starting and running your own business changes you and it's very hard to then change back. It's very hard to decrease the value you yourself put on running your own business and being successful at it, and then return again to put value in things that are ultimately more important, i.e. your health and family for example.

So many people think or say they are doing everything for their children; that they only work to provide for their family and their futures. I would generally tend to doubt this. A successful business owner after about ten or maybe fifteen years should be in a position to walk away after selling up or having invested the profits in other things along the way, and then live off the returns.

The trouble is when you get used to living a certain way and maybe having the latest Italian furniture and perhaps this year's Range Rover and other cars parked in the garage, you also like the treatment that comes with having all these things. The lady of the house likes having the latest fashions to go out in and the guy, well he may like clothes, cars, watches, expensive holidays, who knows.

It's easy to get used to the "high life", especially when you come from more humble upbringings. A bank manager certainly treats you better if they know you are pushing through a decent amount of money each month. A Porsche dealer will treat you quite like an old friend if you are changing you car there every year or so, you may even get on the list for a GT3, but I doubt it. People pay business class prices on airlines to basically get treated like a human being rather than as a chicken in a coop. None of these things matter until you actually have them and get used to them. Speaking from experience, they are indeed nice and they do make you loose site of other things.

You may have walked past business class as you go down the airplane on the way to economy and thought,

"I'd never pay four or five times the price of my ticket just to sit there for eight or nine hours",

And your right, you wouldn't. You could possibly take your whole family on holiday for the price of that one first class ticket. However, when your income is at another level and you travel a lot more, and perhaps you get a free upgrade, then you can easily get used to these luxuries. The problem is then going back and doing without them.

So in order to decide what to do next, you must evaluate what you have and what's really important to you. There are people who need the adrenalin rush of running and being involved in business and without this they feel as if they are nothing, they are also perhaps easily bored and don't know how to relax. Maybe they're really not capable of enjoying themselves with their family and even less so alone. If this is the case, they are probably going to want to work forever, which their families will not appreciate, but as I said, having a business changes you.

If on the other hand you can value other things in life and maybe you even want to get into philanthropy, then there will be many ways for you to occupy your time and your money. I personally think successful businesspersons should, at some stage, give back to their communities; to the planet. I don't think anyone's mission in life should be to leave a fortune to his or her children. I don't say leave them destitute either, but I say live and enjoy your life with them, who knows, there may only be one life to enjoy.

Starting Another Business

If after considering the above, the thrill is what you need or maybe you are not actually so financially comfortable yet to retire, even if you wanted to, then yes you can start another business. You may realize several factors along the way though.

One is that you may not now have the same energy as you did when you started your first company; of course this depends how long ago that was. Two, you may not be quite as flexible as you were previously either; this comes back to how you will have changed during the process of starting the first business.

This whole situation can also be similar to marriages or relationships. Once you have had a few long-term relationships or even marriages and now you are getting older, you tend to get more picky, more fussy and stuck in your ways. Really you tend to narrow your tastes and hence become less flexible. You know what you like and what you don't like, they say. If what you liked about your previous partner was how laid back she was, then its highly unlikely you will consider someone quite quick tempered now.

The same can be true in businesses. If your previous business required a lot of hard work, a lot of hours, but the risk was minimum and you felt quite good about that, its unlikely you are going to go into a high risk business now. When you split up from your partner or business, there were more than likely a few reasons for the split and these reasons will be at the forefront of your mind the next time around.

In my case, I think I had had enough of dealing with students, albeit mature students, but still students, with sometimes unrealistic expectations. I had over 2000 customers at one time and had dealt with over probably 20,000 of them during the life of the company. My idea was to move into a business a little less customer orientated, hence I moved into property, hotels and cars.

That was probably a bit extreme, moving from a business with so many customers to a business where only one customer at any one time would make a purchase. I missed dealing with my customers in the end and ultimately I had become successful, as I was good at that part. However, I was trying to perhaps gain a little less profit, but a little more stability.

The car business I got involved in was really just out of boredom as we have seen and I would definitely warn against such pass times. Don't start any further business ventures just as its something to do, at least not unless you do it alone or there is zero investment involved. I would compare it to splitting up after a long-term relationship and moving in with someone else almost straight away.

In fact, if we stick along this comparison, when you do leave your first business venture and if it was something you did for a good few years, then its best to wait. Rushing into anything else is almost like going on a rebound relationship and they generally don't work out. Be patient, wait for the right opportunity and try recognize even more so this time just what your skill set is.

In my case I felt my very original idea was not a good one, but developing the idea as well as convincing my customers of its worth was my skill set. Business development and sales is pretty much what I had done in my previous career, so perhaps it should not have come as so much of a surprise to learn I was quite good at it. I am not an overbearing person and in general I am quite easy to get on with and that's good for a sales role and for being at the front of any company. If you can make good business relationships, this is a big plus for your company.

Learning From Your Mistakes

If you are going to give it another go and start a second company, you must take something with you from your previous experience. Maybe like me you found yourself spending a lot of time trying to keep an eye on everything. Maybe you even tried, like me, to do too many things yourself, the flyers, website, customer service, sales etc.

Certainly there is no need to go spending a fortune this time, but hopefully you can do things a little better and get the right people in to spread the workload. If money is tight, then you can perhaps offer an interest in the company, or look for people just starting out in their careers, or even students, looking for work experience. There will be designers without much work experience who need to get some projects under their belts in order to fish bigger clients, these will come cheaper.

If you are brave, you can use the numerous websites which offer designers and programmers from all over the world, although mainly India and eastern Europe, who will work for you and your project much cheaper than professionals in your own country no doubt. However, having used these services myself, they certainly have their downfalls. Yes you can have skype conversations, but it's never quite the same as sitting down with the person next to you, no matter what people may say.

What I would say is that you pay for what you get. Certainly you should try to maximize the value for money aspect and I would look at all options, including this one, but just perhaps don't tie yourself to any deadlines with providers or investors if you are relying on people you have never met. You don't know what other projects they are working on and if they get sick, they wont have the back up of fellow staff to help them.

If however you are in no big rush and have plenty of time to get things right, then these more inventive options can save you money and you are still getting high quality results. In general I would say I'd prefer to get someone local who needs the work and experience and is happy to give you a much better price than normal.

If you had a bad partner experience as I did, then maybe you can now be brave enough to go it alone as I also did, especially if you are staying in the same industry and have the experience. Or maybe you tried it alone last time and whether it worked or not, now you might want to start with someone, a problem shared is a problem halved they say.

Another common mistake is to be very trusting with your finances, especially cash that enters the business. It's hard to keep track of everything in a business and well, you need to trust people, but at the same time you need to have controls in place. I am generally pretty lapse with having these controls and I prefer to think of people being honest rather than dishonest. Without going into cultural excuses, I have mixed experiences with trusting people with money and with many things to be honest.

We wont get into details, but the safest and most professional approach is not to leave any temptation in place and to put in as many controls as reasonable. Its better to wish you hadn't than to wish you had in this case. What if the person handling your money is off sick for a few days, they wont want to be responsible for someone else now handling this side of things if there are no controls in place.

Before starting your new business maybe you can make a list of all the things you would do differently after your previous business experience and well now is the perfect time to implement the changes on this list. If you are really going to do this again, do it right!

Do You Need an MBA?

This is not quite the right place for this or even the right book for this, but it's interesting to think about for some of you. First of all I can say NO is the simple answer to this question. In my experience very few entrepreneurs go to school in order to do an MBA before then going on to start their own business. There will of course be those that do, but after having attended and met many thousands of MBA students, I would say the vast majority of full time MBA students start an MBA as their careers have become stagnant and they want to change direction; they think the MBA certificate will help them.

There are an awful lot of people on every MBA course that come from engineering backgrounds, or finance, or law and they honestly feel they will now study for between twelve and twenty four months and with this they will move into their dream job in more than likely the field of marketing. Everyone wants to be in marketing, its quite incredible, it really is.

People think that even with no marketing experience, and instead just having experience of having run a nitric acid plant or been a junior manager in a large accountancy firm, they can compete with people that have been working in marketing for ten to twenty years. And all this bearing in mind that marketing is probably only at best a 10% part of the MBA course content and everything you learn on your MBA is totally theoretical, there is no real life work experience gained at school, not unless you go and do an internship.

Now before the exceptions to the rule are up in arms, yes I have seen some get what they wanted, but they were either very well connected or very lucky, for most of us ugly engineers, there is no easy way out of our industry, unless we perhaps start our own business! So save your money, invest your 50 – 200,000 US$ in your business, not in your MBA.

Well, in truth, running a business is not for everyone either. However, if it is what you are looking at, then you could look at doing many other courses rather than an MBA, where the course content on being an entrepreneur will be even less than the 10% on marketing and I would say many MBA's don't even have any course content relating to starting your own business at all.

An MBA really is more for someone looking to climb the corporate ladder. In fact, for some positions, many higher grade ones, the company will often stipulate as a requirement an MBA, as if those with an MBA are of a different breed. It's almost like an MBA is equivalent to speaking another language when you are applying for a job in another country, like France for example and having an MBA is like being able to speak French.

I am no one to say whether this is right or wrong, but I'd like to say I would hire someone with or without an MBA and would base my decision on their experience and personal characteristics, which, its true, are certainly hard to learn in an interview of course!

There are many short marketing, accounting and even management courses you can do if you feel you are lacking in these areas and if you feel they are important for you when starting a business. I see no harm in this and you can perhaps make some good contacts, which is another reason for doing an MBA of course. There are many companies that actually look for graduates from certain schools. However, I still maintain, you really need more determination, luck and imagination to be able to start your business than an MBA, but if you are unsure what to do in your career as I was, then it's a good experience.

Finally, as I have mentioned before, at the various business clubs you can join you will meet people who can advise and assist and perhaps give you the confidence you need to take the leap and start your own business. Reading this book is perhaps just part of that confidence building process which I am trying to do here.

Can You Really Retire Now?

Well now, this is the million-dollar question in more ways than one. We can tackle it from a financial point of view, but also from a personal point of view. Certainly you need your savings, but also, are you the sort of person to ever retire?

On the personal side first, we have all seen someone we know get to retirement age, take their pension, or even take early retirement, and then this person changes quite dramatically. Unfortunately it's not usually a good change we see, although I am sure there are exceptions. Retired people can tend to get old before they are old and they soon find themselves turning into grumpy old men, complaining about kids running across their lawns or the noises the bin men make, or the lateness of the postman.

When you are not working you naturally have more time to think about these quite irrelevant things, things that would hardly have entered your head before. Your mind would then have been far more occupied with when "the APG order will be ready for shipment", or the latest communication with the Inland Revenue office.

Besides this, you would hope there are people at work with whom you get on with, whether it is your own company or not. You should get some enjoyment out of going to work, maybe not as much as Google's workers, but some enjoyment none the less. This in itself helps you get through the days and helps to keep you good humored, even when back at home maybe.

When you have retired and lost all this, you are basically at home far more, without forcing yourself to get out, or book a cruise. It's quite natural that your mind changes. You will miss the daily activities you had; you will also miss the adrenaline we mentioned above. We also mentioned the sense of importance that is now also gone.

Another thing now, which will be quite new for some people, will be that they are now with their life partners and not business partners or employees, much more than before and this can be a challenge also. There are certainly those relationships that perhaps work, or maybe survive is a better word, because they are quite distant from each other. With the business taking up a lot of their time, there would have been less time than in a normal relationship to spend with your life partner, at least this would be the case for the dedicated business person.

Now that there are no external factors keeping you apart, day and night you will be mainly with your partner. In some cases, this is enough of a reason to not want to retire isn't it? Okay, that's the worse case scenario and certainly not the romantic relationship I would wish for you.

In this more ideal and romantic case, at last you can enjoy your life. Everything you have been waiting for and working for can now be done, although I am not sure why you have waited so long. You can play with your children and see them grow up if they are not already adults by now. If they are adults, well grandchildren will soon follow. The travelling the world plan, sipping coffee in a foreign cafe at a beautiful plaza, watching the beautiful people walk by, can now be fulfilled.

On the money side, which perhaps is what stops people more than anything else, things really depend on your exact situation, your needs and your ideas. If you don't have children or they are now grown up, then your calculations should be a great deal easier than if you have yet to put your children through their schooling.

I became friends with an American petroleum engineer who said he felt he needed about four million dollars to retire, however, the numbers he used were very cautious. He had two daughters who were still at university, but not that far off finishing. The numbers that took me back the most were his "cancer funds".

In most countries, your private health care often does not cover you against cancer and well; cancer is probably the biggest killer out there. On top of that, the treatments for it are also very expensive. So my friend had included in his retirement pot about one million dollars for him and his wife to be treated if the worst ever happened.

I think that's prudent, but a bit negative at the same time. At that rate, I think none of us would ever retire. Another thing people don't think about is really spending what they have. If I have a five bedroom "family" property worth about 1.5 million US$ lets say, then when I am 75 years old I believe I personally would be happy to downsize to an apartment one third of that size and more than likely one third of the value. The apartment will be easier to upkeep and cheaper to maintain also.

That gives me an extra million dollars to spend and enjoy or cover me for a lot of hopefully not needed medical treatments. Some people want to pass their family home to their children, but in reality, it will then just be sold and never used by your family again anyway. Hence, if you want to leave them a nest egg, better leave them cash and better still, leave them what you don't manage to spend. In fact, better yet, leave them great memories, spend your money with them, enjoy! This is surely what you have worked all these years for isn't it?

I have no plans to work all my life and then leave most of what I have saved to my children so they simply don't have to work as hard as I did or they live in a larger property and have a nicer car than I did for example. I think that's truely ridiculous. I'd far rather enjoy my time with and without them than worry about them having these material things when I'm gone, but each to their own.

If you want to work until you're fifty, sixty and even older, just so perhaps your children have an extra bedroom and a Tesla instead of Ford, then so be it, but they wont really thank you for it. In fact, if you spoke to them, they would be pretty mean and badly brought up children if they did not want you to have and enjoy as long as a retirement as possible!

So there I leave you. I hope this book has in an informal way has made you see that you don't need to be so special to start your own business. You don't need an expensive or prolonged education. What you need is some kind of an idea, a great deal of desire, determination and imagination in being able to develop that idea into something workable.

Remember, in the worst case you will fail, but even if you fail, you will in many ways have succeeded!

www.ingramcontent.com/pod-product-compliance
Lightning Source LLC
Chambersburg PA
CBHW051316220526
45468CB00004B/1369